SCREW YOUR WEDDING

A candid guide to wedding planning by a jaded event planner

By Samantha Bellinger

191 Bank Street
Burlington, Vermont 05401

Copyright © 2019 by Samantha Bellinger

All rights reserved. No part of this publication may be reproduced, distributed, or transmitted in any form or by any means, including photocopying, recording, or other electronic or mechanical methods, without the prior written permission of the publisher, except in the case of brief quotations embodied in critical reviews and certain other noncommercial uses permitted by copyright law.

Onion River Press
191 Bank Street
Burlington, VT 05401

Printed in the United States of America

ISBN: 978-1-949066-22-7

Library of Congress Control Number: 2019907499

Table Of Contents

Welcome…	5
How to Use This Book…	7
The 9-Step Process	9
1) Identify The Purpose	10
2) Brainstorm The Basics	11
3) Set Your Budget	14
4) Determine the Date and Location	20
5) Choose Vendors	28
Baker	29
Bar	41
Caterer	54
Florist	62
Music	70
Officiants	81
Photographer	84
Rental Company	97
Stationery	111
Videographer	113
Permits/Licenses	117
Vendor Wrap Up	118
6) Communicate with Guests	119
7) Design the Look	140
8) Create a Day-Of Timeline	183
9) Post-Event Wrap-Up	202
Wrap Up of the Wrap Up	218

 ## Welcome

Hi, I'm Samantha Bellinger, an award-winning event planner with over 10 years of experience.

My event experience has run the gamut. Planning a fundraising event that brought in thousands of dollars with an event budget of zero? Coordinating a multi-day wedding celebration that involved a 25-page event plan? Running a Halloween event for 2000-3000 people while in full costume? I've done it (see below for photo proof). Nothing surprises me anymore.

While my background is varied, I focus on wedding planning. It is by far one of the most complex parts of the event industry. Why? Because it is set up to make couples fail.

That is why I help people planning their wedding cut through the industry jargon and streamline the planning process with my super simple, easy-to-follow 9-step formula.

My advice has been responsible for helping countless people plan the events of their dreams. Now it is available to you in the following pages.

Without this information, there is a good chance you'll suffer from the feelings of stress many experience during the wedding planning process.
With this guide, you'll approach the planning process with confidence — knowing exactly what to do and how to do it — so that you can get married without all the added stress.

That said, it is going to be hard work. You can't just wish your way to success. So get ready to plan like a pro.

Best Wishes,
Samantha

 # How to Use This Book

This book isn't a wedding planning book in the traditional sense.

First, it won't sell you on all the things you should have. It does NOT take a 'you only live once' approach. Instead, it provides a candid, real look at the wedding planning industry and cuts through all that frilly BS.

Second, it recognizes that there is no "one fits all" type of wedding. That is why the process has been designed to be so adaptable.

Finally, this methodology can be modified to plan almost any event. The same 9-step process can be applied to your event.

The content is arranged based on the 9 steps of the planning process. It walks you through a streamlined planning process in order. That said, it is not a book that requires you to start at the top of the Table of Contents and work your way through to the end, although that may not be a bad idea.

The book ends with a section on associated events and helpful timelines you can use as a guide when planning

Happy Planning!

 # The 9-Step Process

Event planners plan weddings a bit differently than DIYers. They simplify. Like, really, really, really over-simplify the process. Honestly, I take it one step at a time. Want to know my process? Read on...

1. Identify The Purpose
2. Brainstorm The Basics
3. Set Your Budget
4. Determine the Date and Location
5. Choose Vendors
6. Communicate with Guests
7. Design the Look
8. Create a Day-Of Timeline
9. Post-Event Wrap-Up

 **Identify The Purpose**

My guess is that if you are reading this your event is a wedding and your goal is to celebrate getting married to your new spouse with your friends and family. Good news... you have the first step already done.

1) The first step is to determine the type of event. I'm guessing yours is a wedding. ;)

2) You also need to determine your target audience. For you, it'll be you, your future spouse, and any family/friends you wish to include.

Combine those two elements to get the purpose of your event. It should be something like this: "My wedding is to celebrate getting married to my future spouse surrounded by our family and friends."

That was easy! Check it off the list >>>

 2 Brainstorm the Basics

Think big picture: the approximate number of guests, general location, feel of the event, etc.

For example, do you want a 500-person wedding in a hotel or a 30-person wedding on an exotic beach?
Don't worry. Nothing needs to be set in stone right now. These just need to be general guidelines to help you in the next few steps.

Consider these questions

1) Where is the ideal ceremony?
In your place of worship? Your backyard? A snowy mountain top? At the courthouse?

2) What does your perfect reception look like?
In a large, posh hotel ballroom with a formal sit-down dinner? Outside under a tent dancing the night away? Having dinner at your favorite restaurant with a few friends?

3) Who would you love to celebrate with?
Your family? Closest friends? Everyone you know?

4) How big is your wedding?
Just a handful of people? Your nearest and dearest? Moderately sized with good friends and close family? Large with all your extended family, friends, and acquaintances?

Brain Dump

Feeling stuck with your brainstorming? Try brain dumping. Brain dumping is when you write down everything that comes into your head. **There are no bad ideas at this point.** Write down EVERYTHING. I mean it.

Step 1 Set a timer for 10 minutes (it can be your phone, microwave, oven, egg timer... doesn't matter how. Just give yourself 10 minutes).

Step 2 Think of "your wedding" and go. Write down or sketch out whatever comes into your head.

Step 3 Step 3: Write down EVERYTHING!

Once the timer goes off, take a break. When you have more time, sit down with your future spouse and evaluate that list. Cross out the things that are absolute "no" items and star the absolute "yes" items. This will give you both an idea of where you overlap and your shared vision for your wedding.

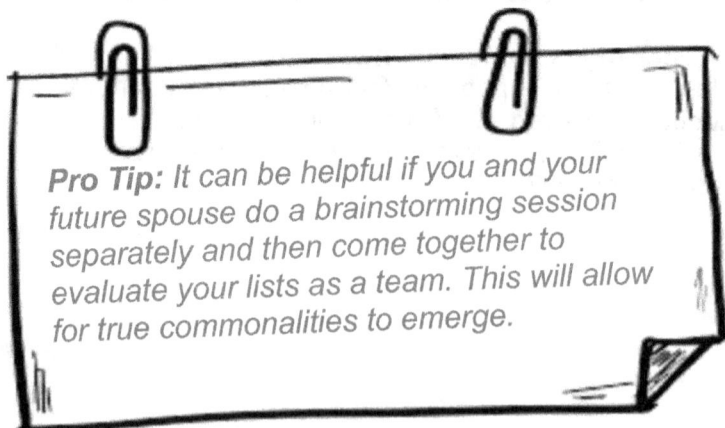

Pro Tip: It can be helpful if you and your future spouse do a brainstorming session separately and then come together to evaluate your lists as a team. This will allow for true commonalities to emerge.

Decide

By the end of this section you should have agreed upon a general idea. You need to know:

Size

Decide on the size. Try to be as specific as possible. Don't worry about having to finalize the guest list yet. Just determine the approximate size. It can be a range (i.e. 75-100).

Number of Guests: _____

Location

Decide on the general location. By this I mean the region of the world you want to concentrate on. Think city, state, and country.

Sometimes this is an easy decision. It can be where you grew up or where you live now. Or it can be a destination wedding anywhere in the world. You choose.

Location: _____

 ## Set Your Budget

Budgets can cause stress for some people. Make it easy on yourself. Use the budget template on page 14 to outline projected expenses. Be realistic with this!

Regardless of your budget, it is important to determine what you are comfortable spending up front. This means a base line and then set aside some of that money for unexpected costs/expenses.

> IF YOU ARE PLANNING TO GET MARRIED, BE REALISTIC ABOUT WHAT YOU CAN AFFORD TO PAY FOR YOUR WEDDING.

Let's Talk Money: Budget Conversations
Talking about money can be uncomfortable. However, it is an important conversation with wedding planning.

Figure out who is paying for what. Are you covering the majority of the expenses? Is anyone else contributing? If so, what are they contributing? Not sure? Ask!

WEDDING BUDGET

HOW TO USE: This is a sample budget with percentages. These are the average percentages a couple sends on any given category. Apply the percentages to your own overall budget for a good starting point.

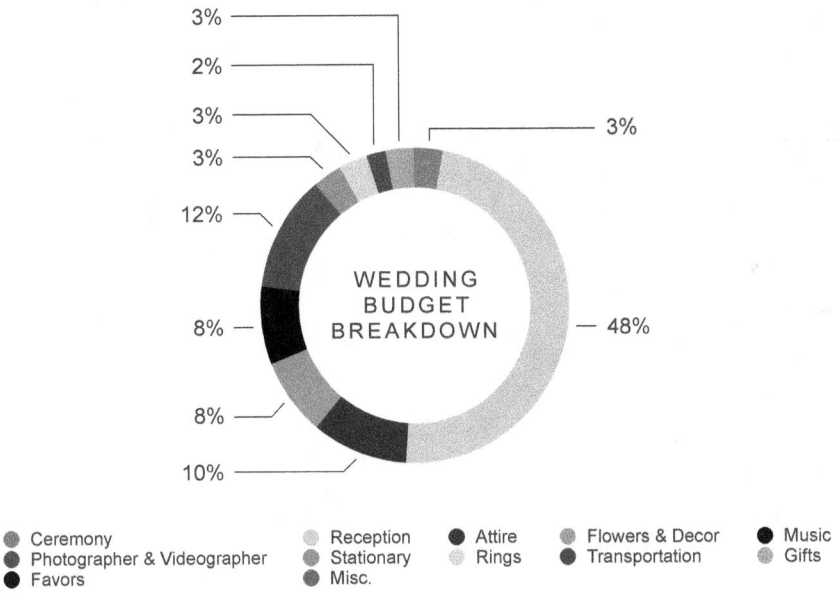

- Ceremony
- Photographer & Videographer
- Favors
- Reception
- Stationary
- Misc.
- Attire
- Rings
- Flowers & Decor
- Transportation
- Music
- Gifts

SUMMARY BY CATEGORY

Category	Budget	Actual	Difference
Ceremony	3%		
Location fee			
Officiant Fee/Donation			
Decorations/Accessories			
Reception	48%		
Venue			
Rentals			
Food/Catering Service			
Alcohol/Bar Service			

Category	Budget	Actual	Difference
Cake/Cutting Fee			
Attire		10%	
Partner 1			
Outfit			
Shoes			
Accessories			
Alterations			
Partner 2			
Outfit			
Shoes			
Accessories			
Alterations			
Flowers & Decor		8%	
Ceremony Site Decor			
Bouquets/Boutonnieres			
Centerpieces			
Other Decorations			
Music		8%	
Ceremony			
Cocktail Hour			
Reception			
Other Expenses			
Photographer & Videographer		12%	
Photographer			
Videographer			
Keepsakes (Prints, Videos, Books, etc.)			
Stationary		3%	
Save the Dates			
Invitations			
Reply Cards			
Thank You Notes			

Category	Budget	Actual	Difference
Postage			
Name Cards (Place Cards & Escort Cards)			
Extras: Ceremony Programs, Menus, etc.			
Rings		3%	
Partner 1			
Partner 2			
Transportation		2%	
For Couple			
For Wedding Party			
For Guests			
Gifts		3%	
Each other			
Parents			
Attendants			
Favors			
Misc.			
Total		100%	$0.00

Pay for It Yourself
Many couples pay for the celebration by themselves with no help from anyone. This means only you and your future spouse need to discuss the budget.

Way Back When
Traditional planning books will tell you that the bride's family pays for the majority of the expenses (clothing, reception, etc.) while the groom's family pays for the marriage license, officiant, and rehearsal dinner.

Obviously, this is outdated advice. Only 1-2% of US couples still have the bride's family pay for everything. It is usually a joint family venture or paid for entirely by the couple.

Regardless of your monetary situation, <u>conversations have to be had</u>.

Conversation with Your Partner
What savings do you both have? What are you willing to spend?

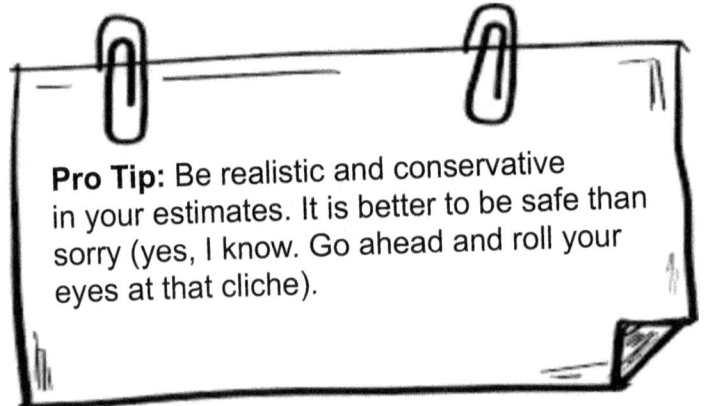

Pro Tip: Be realistic and conservative in your estimates. It is better to be safe than sorry (yes, I know. Go ahead and roll your eyes at that cliche).

Conversation with Family

Are your parents, in-laws, or other family members contributing monetarily to your wedding? If so, how much? When do they plan to contribute?

Pro Tip: Have family members "sponsor" something specific with their monetary contribution. (For example, flowers, food, the photographer, etc.) By being able to pay for something specific, their input can be limited to that thing only. This will avoid needing their approval for every single detail throughout the entire planning process.

4 Determine the Date and Location

For event planners, the next steps are to decide on a date and location. These tasks are usually done together. This means if you book a venue, you have two things done at once.

This process usually takes more than a day, so let me outline the path to that accomplishment.

Step 1 Research the venues that match your requirements (i.e., places in your desired location and have enough space for your approximate guest count). Then shortlist 3-5 places.

Step 2 Contact those shortlisted 3-5 places.

Need a script/template? Use this one:

Subject: Venue Inquiry for [YEAR] Wedding

Hi [VENUE NAME] Team,

I'm at the beginning stages of wedding planning and I am interested in [VENUE NAME] as a possibility for our wedding reception. I'd love to arrange a site visit with you to see the space and chat about what the space has to offer. Would you be available to meet with me in the coming weeks? I'm typically available {DAYS/TIMES OF THE WEEK AVAILABLE]. Before we meet, I figure you probably want to know a little about our wedding, so here are the basics: My FH/FW and I are looking for a venue to hold [APPROX # OF GUESTS]. We don't have a specific date in mind but are hoping for something in [MONTH/SEASON] of [YEAR]. I look forward to talking with you and seeing if we are a good fit.

Thanks for your time,
[FULL NAME]
[PHONE NUMBER]

If you are able to make contact with the venue representative via phone, ask if they have 10 minutes to answer your questions. Use the *Venue Checklist* to narrow down your list of acceptable venues. You can also have this conversation during your site visit.

Questions:

1. How close is the venue to your other locations (hotels, ceremony site, etc.)?
2. Is the space available on the desired date/time? Or what are the open dates?
3. What is the price?
4. Are there discounts for other days of the week or off-season?
5. What does that price include?
6. What is the venue capacity? How many people can the space comfortably hold? Note: capacity will be different depending on whether people are seated, standing, or a combination of both.
7. Are there separate spaces for the different types of activities you may be (or may not be) hosting? Meaning cocktails, eating, dancing, etc.
8. What are the venue's policies and contractual language on refunds, guarantees, and liability in case of cancellation, damage, etc.?
9. Does the venue have on-site catering? If so, are you required to use them? What are the menus? Are there food and drink minimums? If so, what are they?
10. If not, do they have a preferred vendor list? Can you use vendors not on the list?

11. Do they allow outside vendors (i.e. vendors not supplied by them and/or not on their preferred list)? If so, is there an approval process for outside vendors?
12. What is the reputation of the venue? Have they had any recent issues that would give people pause? You can do this by researching customer reviews on websites like Yelp and/or searching for the venue on google?
13. Are there any weather issues that might interfere with the event? (For example, rain for an outdoor ceremony). If so, what are the backup solutions?
14. What kind of heating/cooling systems does the space have? Can they reliably create a comfortable environment regardless of the weather that day?
15. Is there adequate light? Is there natural light? Is there a way to shade the sun if necessary?
16. Where are the outlets? How many are there?
17. Does the space have built-in Audio-Visual (AV) equipment? If so, what kind of equipment is available to use?
18. What kind of personal amplification (PA) and music amplification system does the space have? Is there a specification sheet you could have?
19. Is there a preferred vendor list for music?
20. What bathroom facilities are available?
21. Is there ample parking for the guests?
22. Are there any restrictions that the venue has when renting the space?

Venue Selection

Most couples planning a wedding have never done a site visit before. Venues expect this, so there no reason to be anxious. Seriously, don't worry. A site visit is simply seeing the place and gathering as much information as you can. The key is to make it a conversation. It shouldn't just be them selling the space to you, or you trying to persuade them to take on your event. It should be a chance to discover if it will be mutually beneficial.

Jiving well will make the whole planning process a gazillion times easier.

Instructions

Site visits are generally done before a final decision has been made on the event location. Therefore, the goal of a site visit is to leave with all the technical, operational, and aesthetic information you would need to design and produce your event.

Step 1 Start by contacting the event manager at the venue or whoever they have in charge of this function. Don't worry about their job titles; they will be all over the map. Explain that you are interested in conducting a site visit because you are considering the space for your wedding. Ask to set up a meeting time that is mutually agreeable.

Step 2 Meet with the event manager at the specified day and time. Be sure to be 5 minutes early – not 27 minutes early or 9 minutes late. Event professionals can be obsessive about their time. They will likely start worrying that you are a no show if you are 3 minutes late or annoyed if you show up too early. This isn't because they aren't flexible; they probably have back-to-back meetings or multiple events going on later that day. Event planners typically sprint from one place to another while juggling 17 balls and answering phone calls on the fly. All this to say that you will have a WAY better experience if you show up 5 minutes early to your meeting.

Step 3 Take a tour of the venue/event space. They will be showing you the place and giving you a well-practiced spiel.

Step 4 Ask the manager the series of questions available on page 2. Be sure to go through the entire checklist and record the answers. Even if you don't care about the electrical sockets, chances are that your DJ/Band will ask you about it. It'll save you a lot of back & forth if you get the information now.

Step 5 After the visit, thank the manager for meeting with you. They may become a great resource if you decide to use this space. You'll get better service if you are appreciative of their time from the start.

Step 6 Review the notes you've taken and determine if the venue would be appropriate for your needs. I mean it. Does it comfortably sit 50 for dinner, but your family is gigantic? Don't book it. Does it require you to use their catering services, but you have your heart set on using the restaurant where you two went on your first date? Don't book it. Even if you fell in love with the space, find one that meets your needs.

Step 7 Write a summary of your experience and the information you've collected. This is especially helpful when comparing your list of places.

EVENT SITE INSPECTION CHECKLIST

Event Name:
Venue:

Date & Time of Event:
Set-up Date and Time:
Take-down Date and Time:

Venue Contact:
Name: Phone: Cell: Email:

Contact information for other vendors: *Include name, position, and contact information for each.*

Banquet/Catering   Audio Visual   Engineer
Setup Crew   Security

ARRIVAL - Front door

Distance - how are guests arriving?
First Impressions
Parking - # of spaces, cost, is valet available
Guest Access to space(s), separate entrance?
Registration / Coat Check

Toilets - location, size, amenities, décor needed?
Pre-function Foyer - is there one, reception suitable, secure/private?
Entrance into Event Space - strong or weak impression, does it lend itself to decorating?

ARRIVAL - Back dock
Ease of Access to Dock
Dock Height
Truck Parking
Security/Dock Control

Dock Supervisor
Access Path to Space:
Distance

Dimensions of smallest door into space
Elevator Dimensions
Delivery Challenges

ROOM SPECS –
get space plan
Floor Plan
Ceiling Plan with Rigging Points
Electrical Plan

Typical Table Layouts
Typical Exhibit Layouts Width & Length of Room(s)
Ceiling Height(s)
Electrical

Storage space
Dressing Rooms
Work Space
Water Access
Trash Disposal

STAGING –
qty. sizes & heights

Steps

Ramp

CATERING - in-house/off premise?
Menus

Specialties

Service Styles

TABLES & CHAIRS
Tables: 60" rd. _____ 66" rd. _____ 72" rd. _____ 8' banquet _____ 6' banquet
Quantity of Banquet chairs   Other Tables - 1/2 rd., cocktail & highboys

MISCELLANEOUS
Glassware   Flatware   Linens   Amenities – lecterns, podiums, easels, stanchions, etc.

 **Vendors**

This step includes any vendors you might want to hire. It could include a caterer, bar, bakery, DJ/Band, officiant, flowers, photographer, videographer, etc. You can hire all of these, none of these, or somewhere in between. It is your day. You do what is right for you.

Regardless of which ones you choose to invest in, there are helpful resources (questions to ask, email templates to use, etc.) under each of the sections.

Please notes that the vendor section is organized alphabetically. This way you can flip directly to your desired vendor type for more information.

Baker

One of the things that always fascinates me is what people decide to do for their 'cake.' When I first started in the wedding industry, it was almost always a white frosted cake in varying sizes. Today it could be a colorful, themed fondant cake, a cupcake tree, a full candy bar, or a strategically arranged stack of donuts. I've even seen an ice cream truck pull up for the "cake cutting" ceremony.

Yet when most people think wedding, they think of a large white multi-tiered cake. That image has been etched into the collective mind of society along with big poofy white dresses and flower bouquets. However, that cliched idea doesn't mean you need a multi-tiered cake.

Given the invite possibilities, I've structured this chapter in three sections: 1) Hiring a professional baker for a cake; 2) Alternatives to Cake; 3) Doing it Yourself. Flip to whichever section you think you will find most helpful. Or read them all to help you decide.

Professional Baker:
If you choose to have cake and use a baker, I recommend finding someone who fits your style well. Want a down-to-earth cake that seems like grandma made it? Don't go with the baker who is well-known for their fondant masterpieces.

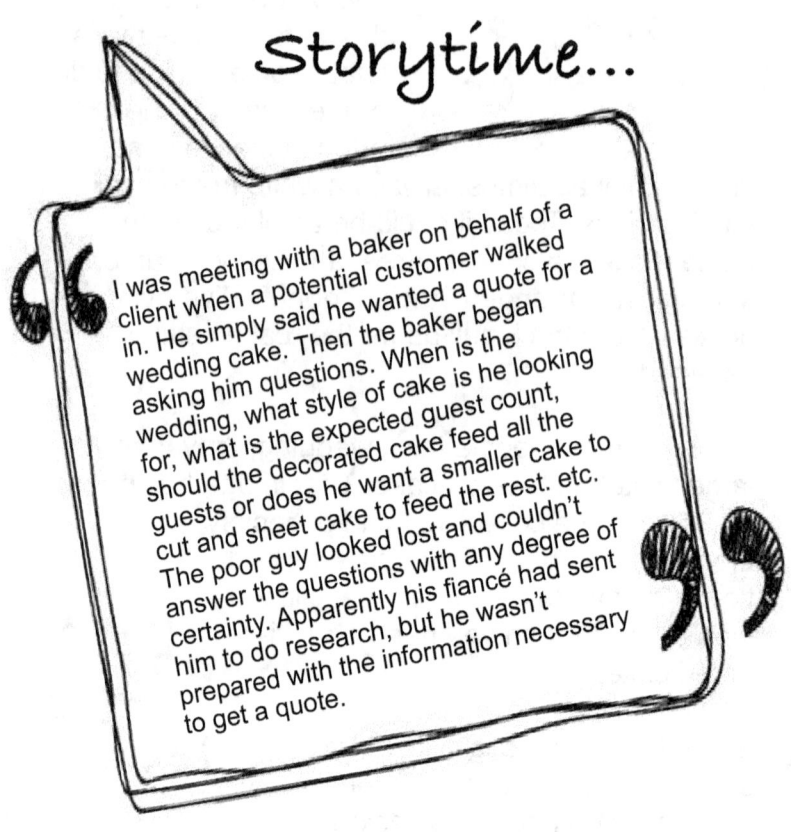

Storytime...

"I was meeting with a baker on behalf of a client when a potential customer walked in. He simply said he wanted a quote for a wedding cake. Then the baker began asking him questions. When is the wedding, what style of cake is he looking for, what is the expected guest count, should the decorated cake feed all the guests or does he want a smaller cake to cut and sheet cake to feed the rest. etc. The poor guy looked lost and couldn't answer the questions with any degree of certainty. Apparently his fiancé had sent him to do research, but he wasn't prepared with the information necessary to get a quote."

To avoid this embarrassment and the frustration of wasting time, I recommend doing some prep work prior to contacting a baker.

First, do your research. Then shortlist the bakers to your top 3-5 choices.

Email those bakers with the following useful information:
1. Date of Wedding (include the year too!)

2. Location of the wedding reception
3. Expected number of guests
4. Any guidance on what you are looking for in terms of style, flavors, etc.
5. Finish the email with a request for a quote and/or setting up a consultation or tasting. Be sure to ask their policy on tastings (if they are included in the price or require a fee).

Email Template

Hi [Insert Name or Company Name],

I hope you are doing well. [Insert how you heard about them: I was impressed by your cakes at an event I attended / a friend recommended you]. I'm reaching out to discuss the possibility of you baking the cake for my wedding.

Here are the event details:
[Month Date, Year] Wedding at [Venue Name, Town, State]. We expect there to will be around [Approx. number of people] guests.

I'm looking for a [Cake description such as cake to cut and sheet cake to serve]. We are looking for someone who is able to provide [additional cake descriptors such as flavors or style].

Please let me know if you are available for [Wedding Date] and, if so, an initial quote. If all is good from there, I'd like to set up an in-person meeting to discuss details further.

I look forward to hearing from you,
[Your Name]
[Your Contact Information]

Lingo Decoding

It is also helpful to determine your desired style and what you think you want. Every vendor in the wedding industry has their own jargon. For help with that, let's decode some of the common lingo.

Icings

Buttercream and Fondant are the two most common icings used for wedding cakes. To make the determination easier, I've included a chart of the pros/cons of each *(see next page)*

- **Buttercream** is rich and creamy (it is almost made entirely out of butter). It is easily colored, flavored, and used for simple decoration (flowers, etc.).

    Forewarning: While it is delicious, buttercream has a tendency to melt in extreme heat. Therefore, it's not recommended for outdoor summer weddings in the American South.

- **Fondant** is smooth and stiff and provides for an incredible appearance. It is made with gelatin and corn syrup, which allows it to be intricately decorated (it does not require refrigeration). However, the taste is severely lacking.

- **Ganache** is a thick dark icing made from chocolate and heavy cream. It has a similar consistency of store-bought chocolate icing, but the taste is worlds better. However, it also requires a temperature-controlled climate. Avoid using it in hot or humid weather or the icing will slide right off the cake.

- **Royal Icing** is the white icing they use on gingerbread. It is a mix of confectioner's sugar and milk or egg whites. It is mostly used for more delicate decoration work (lattice, lace, dots, etc.). It also has the perk of not need to be refrigerated.

- **Whipped Cream** looks beautiful and tastes great. Yet it is typically avoided with wedding cakes because they tend to be out of the fridge for so long. If you do use whipped cream, make sure your cake is in the fridge until the very last possible second.

Buttercream vs. Fondant

	Pros	Cons
FONDANT	Easy to work with	The taste can be mediocre
	Versatile	
	Fashion-forward	
BUTTERCREAM	Creamy	Doesn't hold up well in sun or heat
	Delicious	Not as eye-popping as fondant
	Old-fashioned elegance	

- Arrange a consultation with your potential cake designer in person, and do a tasting before you sign a contract.

- Not all cake tastings are complimentary. Some will ask you to pay and then apply that cost towards your final bill once you sign a contract.

- Make sure your cake designer specializes in wedding cakes. A wedding cake is generally much more elaborate than a birthday cake from your local bakery. Your cake professional should have special training in constructing this type of cake.

- In general, you should order your cake six to eight months prior to your wedding.

- You might be able to save money by choosing one overall flavor for your cake or by having a small cake for display and the cake cutting accompanied by a sheet cake to serve to your guests.

- If you plan to save the top tier of your cake, let your baker know so they can give you a box, and don't forget to tell your caterer to put it aside!

Questions to ask a professional baker
I've seen a lot of brides freeze before their first consultation with the baker. They are stumped on what they should be asking to make sure they have the best experience. To help you know what to consider when chatting with bakers, I've compiled a list of common questions you should consider.

Determining Fit:
- Are you licensed and insured?
- Do you have a portfolio of past designs we can look at?
- Have you ever done a cake similar to mine, if so can we see examples?
- Is there a set selection of designs to choose from or do you create completely custom cakes? If you have some standard cakes? What are their prices?
- We saw some ideas on Pinterest. Can you create a similar style?
- We have no idea what we'd like! Can you offer some design suggestions based on our budget and theme?
- Can you provide a few references?

Availability:
- Do you have my wedding date open?
- How many wedding cakes do you typically schedule on the same day? How many is your max? *Tip*: You want to feel comfortable that your designer is sufficiently staffed to handle the number of cakes they've scheduled to deliver and set up on your date.

Renting:
- Can we rent display items from you? If so, what do you have available to rent (cake stands, toppers, cake knives, etc.)? What are the fees for each of these?
- If we are renting items from you, how and when should they be returned?
- How will the cake be displayed? Do you provide or rent cake stands? Do you decorate the cake table too?

Ordering Logistics:
- What size and shape should the tiers be to feed our guest list? How big should our cake be?
- How far in advance do I need to order my cake?
- When does my order need to be finalized? If you need a headcount, when do you need it?

Flavor:
- What cake flavors do you offer? How about filling flavors?
- Do you have set flavor combinations? Or can we mix-and-match?
- • What flavors are your specialties?
- What kinds of ingredients do you use? Do you offer organic, vegan, or gluten-free options?
- Are your cakes finished in buttercream or with fondant?

Tastings:
- Is a tasting included in our fee? If not, how much will it cost? *
- Will you do a tasting consultation, or will we simply be tasting the cake on our own? *

Price:
- How do you price your cakes? By the slice? Does the cost vary depending on the design and flavors I choose? *

- Do you have a minimum cost? Is there a base fee?
- Can you realistically work within my budget? If so, what will it look like?
- What recommendations can you give me to maximize my budget?
- Is there a delivery fee?
- Are there additional rental fees we should be aware of, such as for cakes stands, cake toppers, or cake knives?
- How much is the deposit? When is it due?
- When is final payment due?
- What is your refund policy if we need to cancel our order?
- When should we expect to receive a contract?

Delivery:
- What delivery services do you offer?
- How do you deliver the cake? What do you do if it is damaged in transit? *

Pro tip: Many bakers do charge a fee for a cake tasting, but will then apply that amount toward the final cost of your cake if you sign a contract.

Pro tip: Some bakers will do a consultation that includes a tasting of a number of flavors, plus a discussion of your cake design, while others will simply provide you with the flavors for you to taste on your own, then discuss design after you've signed the contract.

Pro tip: Most bakers charge per serving, meaning the price of your cake will depend on how many slices it includes.

Pro tip: Find out when and how your baker will deliver your cake, and make sure the cake table is set up before he or she arrives.

Doing it Yourself

Don't want to work with a baker? No problem. You can always DIY the cake. You can do this by baking things yourself, purchasing them from a grocery store/discount store, having family/friends help, etc. Here are some things to consider:

<u>Baking it Yourself</u>
Nothing beats a homemade cake (yes, even if it's a box mix). Just be aware that this option might come with some added stress. In order to have a fresh delicious cake you will need to wait to bake the cake in the day or two before the wedding. You'll already be running around doing 500 last minute things, half of which you weren't expecting. Just something to consider.

<u>Having Friends/Family Help</u>
Want your cake homemade but don't want to do it all yourself? Enlist your family and friends to help. They can each bake one cake or two dozen cupcakes. Think of it like a potluck, but with only baked goods.

<u>Purchasing Cake</u>
You can buy large sheet cakes and/or cupcakes from the grocery store or a large discount store (Costco, Sam's Club, etc.). You can have it personalized or not. Regardless, it doesn't have to be fancy.

<u>Determining Cake Amounts</u>
If you are DIYing this portion, you'll need to know how to determine the amount of cake you need to bake/buy.

Determining Cake Amounts
How Much Do You Really Need?

Industry standards suggest 1 serving per person, plus 30% extra of each.

Serving Sizes:

1 slice of Cake, Tart or Pastry
4 oz. Pudding/Mouse
2 scoops of Ice Cream

When serving two of the above, reduce each by half.

What that looks like:

192 servings (1 in x 2 in) per full sheet cake
108 servings (1 in x 2 in) per half size sheet cake
54 servings (1 in x 2 in) per quarter sheet size cake

117 servings (2 in x 2 in) per full sheet cake
54 servings (2 in x 2 in) per half size sheet cake
24 servings (2 in x 2 in) per quarter sheet size cake

6-8 servings per 6 inch round cake
10-14 servings per 8 inch round cake
20-25 servings per 10 inch round cake
25-35 servings per 12 inch round cake
35-45 servings per 14 inch round cake
45-55 servings per 16 inch round cake

6-8 servings per 9 inch pie or tart

32 scoops per 1 gallon container of ice cream
64 scoops per 2 gallon container of ice cream
96 scoops per 3 gallon container of ice cream

Alternatives to Cake
No one says you HAVE to have cake. There are plenty of alternatives. Consider some of these other options:

- Pies
- Cupcakes
- Doughnuts
- Rice Krispie Treats
- Candy
- Ice Cream (either cake form or scooped)
- Cake Pops
- Macaroons
- Various baked goods
- Anything else you can think of...

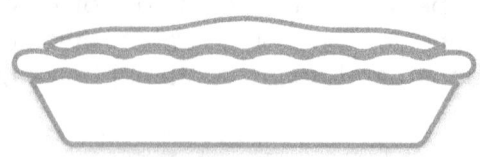

 Welcome to the section on how to either prevent or encourage drunken shenanigans (it's your choice).

So let's talk about choosing a bar service that is right for you and your wedding. Your options will vary depending on your location, your local liquor laws, and any restrictions or requirements that your venue may have.

In the next few sections, I'm going to outline a few common approaches for wedding bar services.

Hiring a Professional Bar Service
If you're in the US, some states and venues require a licensed, insured bar service to serve your guests alcohol. This is certainly the most secure option because bar services in your area will have experience adhering to the local liquor laws. It will eliminate a whole host of worries from your list.

If you want to pursue this option and you're not sure where to start searching for bar services, I would recommend asking your venue if they have a preferred vendor list. This list will have the vendors who regularly work with your venue that are comfortable with the logistical quirks they need to plan for (i.e., needing extra refrigerator space, how close the kitchen is to their set up, the extra equipment they need to bring, etc.)

Once you decide to talk to possible bar services, it is helpful to know what questions to ask before signing a contract. I've compiled a list of 30 questions and 5 pro tips for you to use. This easy-to-use list can be found in the next few pages.

As a bonus, I've also included a ready-for-you email template to get your bar service to respond quickly. All you have to do is copy, paste and fill in the blanks with your information. It'll save you time and get you a higher rate of response from potential vendors.

Email template to get them to respond quickly

> Hi [Vendor's First Name or the Business Name],
>
> I hope you are doing well. I'm writing to you today for a bar quote. I'd love to discuss the possibility of you providing a bar for my own wedding.
>
> Here are the event details:
>
> [Month Date, Year] Wedding at [Venue Name, Town, State]. There will be approximately [#] guests.
>
> I'm looking for a(n) [open/limited/cash] bar with [types of alcohol you want served]. We'd also like to do a self-serve watering station to reroute unnecessary traffic from the bar.
>
> Please let me know if you are available for [Wedding Date] and if so, an initial quote. If all is good from there, I'd like to set up an in-person meeting to discuss details further.
>
> I hope to talk with you soon,
>
> [Your Name & Contact Information]

Questions to Ask the Bartending Service

- Is your bar service licensed? Do you have insurance? Can you provide proof for the venue?
- Are the bartenders they use trained/certified?
- What does the price include (staff, alcohol, drinkware, etc.)?
- Is a liquor license required? If so, are their additional costs associated with it?
- Do we need to purchase separate liability insurance? Or is that included in the service?
- How many bartenders to they recommend for the number of people you expect?
- How many guests are of drinking age? Are bartenders trained in ID checks?
- Is more than one bar needed in order to avoid lines?
- What will happen to leftover alcohol?
- Will they provide a bar menu? If so, how will the bar menu be displayed?
- Are there restrictions on how alcohol can be served? For example, are shots and/or drinking games allowed?
- Will they provide all the alcohol, mixers, and garnishes?

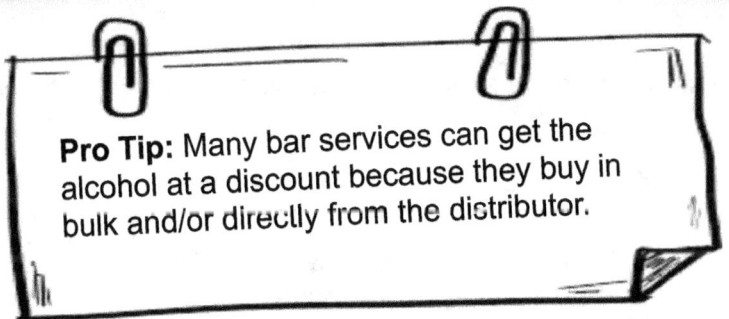

Pro Tip: Many bar services can get the alcohol at a discount because they buy in bulk and/or directly from the distributor.

- What will drinks be served in and can you rent/purchase drinkware from them?
- Will regular non-alcoholic drink service be done at the bar too? Or will there be a self-service area?

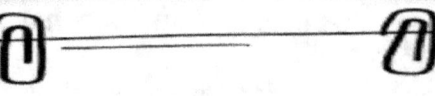

Pro tip: it is a good idea to have a self-serve water station to help minimize the line at the bar.

- Will it be an open bar or cash bar?

Pro Tip: Be aware of the drinking habits of your guests. I've seen some heated family fights over this decision. Regardless of what you choose, just be forewarned there will likely be unsolicited commentary.

- Is self-service allowed at your venue?

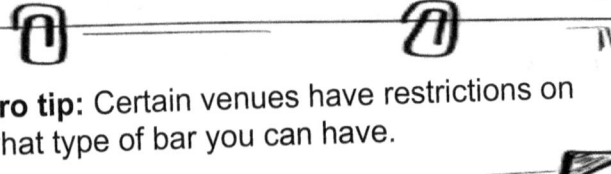

Pro tip: Certain venues have restrictions on what type of bar you can have.

- What type of alcohol will be served?
- Will there be a signature drink for the event?

Pro Tip: Many couples opt for a signature drink (or three) instead of offering a full range of liquors. It can keep the costs lower if done right.

- Who is setting up and breaking down the bar?
- How long does setup and cleanup take? How far in advance does bar staff arrive?
- Where will the bar(s) be located?
- What tables and linens are needed for the bar?
- Who is providing the tables and linens?
- How much ice will be needed? Who is providing the ice? How will the ice be stored?
- How will drinks be chilled and who is responsible?
- Who is responsible for bar trash?
- Does anything need to be rented for the bar? (i.e., drink dispensers, coolers, linens, tables, etc.)
- Will the bartender, bar and/or alcohol need to be relocated during the event? If so, when and where?

Hiring a Bartender
Another popular option is hiring a bartender.

Some states and venues allow you to supply your own alcohol if you hire a trained bartender. This was the case when I lived in Maryland. I bartended numerous parties and weddings for people supplying their own alcohol. You can usually find these through a local bartending school. The schools sometimes have lists of qualified bartenders. Plus it's a much more secure way to find help than on Craigslist.

Before pursuing this option, be sure to check your local liquor laws to see if this is legal in your area.

That's it for now. Up next is an explanation of the self-serve, supply-your-own option.

Supply Your Own
Another popular option for weddings is supplying your own alcohol.

Some states and venues allow you to supply your own alcohol without needing a service or a bartender. You can provide the alcohol and allow people to serve themselves. If you plan to go this route, be sure to research local liquor laws and adhere to all the regulations. You can usually find out more information about liquor laws through the state department of liquor, or another government agency in charge of liquor regulations.

When supplying your own alcohol, you'll need to ask yourself the following questions:

- Do I need liability insurance?
- What is my venue's policy on supplying your own alcohol?
- What type of alcohol are you serving?
- How much of each type of alcohol is needed?
- What amount of non-alcohol drinks, mixers, and garnishes are needed?
- Will there be a champagne toast? If so, how will that work?
- What will drinks be served in? What drinkware needs to be rented or purchased?
- How much ice will be needed? Who is providing the ice? How will the ice be stored?
- How will drinks be chilled and who is responsible for doing so?
- How will the bar(s) be set up and who is responsible for that?
- Will you provide more than one bar station to cut down on lines?
- Is everyone of legal drinking age? If not, who will enforce this?
- What will happen to leftover alcohol?
- Where will the bar(s) be located?
- What tables and linens are needed for the bar? Are you renting or buying them?
- How does clean up work? Who is responsible for that?

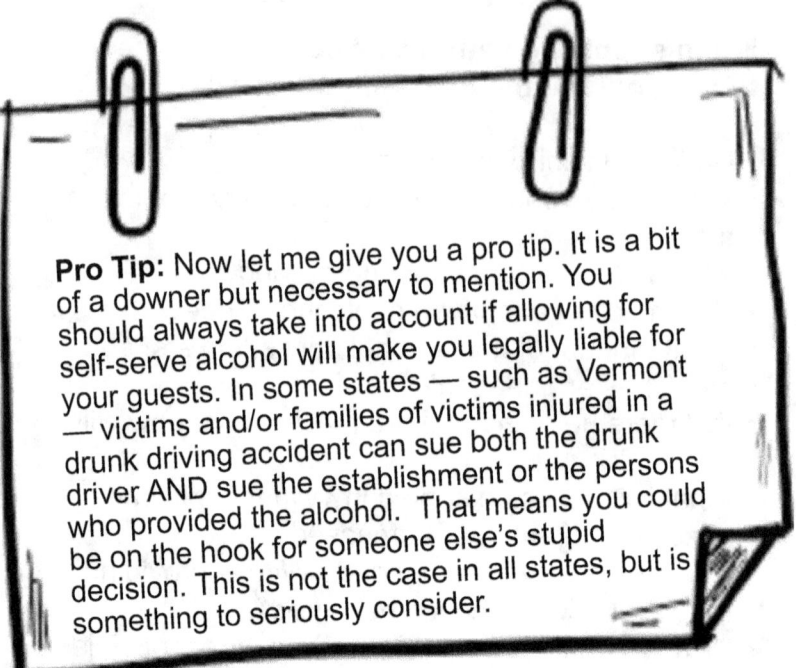

Pro Tip: Now let me give you a pro tip. It is a bit of a downer but necessary to mention. You should always take into account if allowing for self-serve alcohol will make you legally liable for your guests. In some states — such as Vermont — victims and/or families of victims injured in a drunk driving accident can sue both the drunk driver AND sue the establishment or the persons who provided the alcohol. That means you could be on the hook for someone else's stupid decision. This is not the case in all states, but is something to seriously consider.

Now, on to the lighter side of things.

Supplying your own alcohol can save you money in the long run, especially if you purchase all of your alcohol from one supplier.

When you decide to supply your own alcohol, you'll need to ask yourself a few questions. I've compiled a list of 16 helpful questions that you can see on the following pages.

That's it for this section. Up next is an explanation of how to determine the amounts you'll need. I promise you a funny story in that one.

Determining Amounts of Alcohol
If you decide to go with supplying your own alcohol, you'll need to determine how much alcohol you need to purchase.

I have a funny story about this. Actually, it is half hilarity and half cautionary tale.

Storytime...

"A friend of mine got married on his family farm and decided to supply his own alcohol. His soon-to-be wife found helpful diagrams online of how much booze you should purchase. All was going well until...

He applied the suggested amount incorrectly.

He ended up procuring 3 palettes of beer — that's right 3 full palettes — delivered in 2 truck loads. It was 150 cases of beer or 3,600 cans of beer. Now it was a big wedding, but it was not THAT big. It ended up working out to be..."

To help you avoid this error — and have a more reasonable experience — I have included beverage consumption guidelines in a document on the next page.

"14 beers per person. Only it was 14 beers for every man, woman and child... yup... he'd calculated it based on the entire guest count, not just the guests who were drinking. Did I mention there were 75 children and 20 pregnant women?

Yeah... oops!

To make matters worse, he applied the same process to the wine, hard liquor, and non-alcoholic drinks.

Needless to say, it was overkill.

Cases of beer as unexpected party favors? Check!"

...Storytime

Determining Alcohol Amounts
How Much Do You Really Need?

Industry standards suggest 1 serving per person per hour.
Multiple this by the number of hours of the event

Serving Sizes:
4 glasses of wine per bottle
1 drink of beer per bottle
18 drinks of spirits per bottle
165 drinks of beer per keg

Ratios for how much to buy of each type of alcohol:

 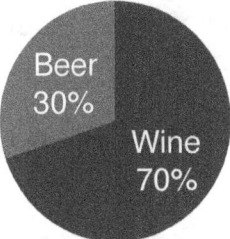

What that looks like:
100 people x 6 hours = 600 servings

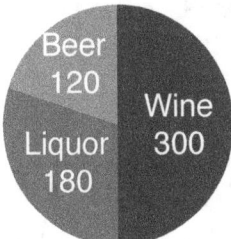 

That translates to:

75 bottles wine   105 bottles of wine
120 bottles beer   180 bottles beer
10 bottle of liquor   (or 1 Keg + 1 case)

When you are buying in bulk, be sure to buy in cases. Many times you'll get a discount for buying by the case.

Types of Bars
To Drink or Not to Drink, That is the Question

Ok, let's talk about the ups and downs of a full bar, limited bar, dry wedding receptions, as well as the open bar vs cash bar debate. The basic definitions:

Full Bar: Almost anything/everything is provided to guests. This means beer, wine, and a large variety of liquors.

Limited Bar: This means a limited selection is provided. One of the most common options is a small selection of wines, a few different beers, and a signature drink involving hard liquor.

Dry Wedding: No alcohol is served

Sample Limited Bar Menu

1 type of Red Wine
1 type of White Wine
2-3 beer options (1 light, 1 lager, & 1 IPA)
Signature Cocktail

Bar Showdown: Full vs. Cash Bar

Be aware of the drinking habits of your guests. I've seen some heated family fights over this decision. In many circles, it is considered "tacky" or "rude" to have a cash bar. That said, some circles expect it and consider it normal. Neither is right or wrong. It is your wedding - do what you deem best. Regardless of what you choose, just be forewarned there will likely be unsolicited commentary.

Open Bar:
The hosts pay for everything without restrictions.

Limited Bar:
Hosts pay for some of the drinks. How would this look? This could be hosts paying for drinks the first few hours the bar is open or hosts pay for beer and wine while guests pay for liquor. Both options provide guests with drinks while limiting the hosts' expenses.

Cash Bar:
This options provides alcohol at the cost of the guests.

Be aware that some venues/bar services will still require hosts to pay a base fee and then will have a

I once had a friend say to me that his dad always said, "the only thing you need for a successful wedding is good food and booze. No one remembers the rest." I couldn't agree more.

It's been three years and people are still talking about how delicious the BBQ (pulled pork for those of you who aren't North Carolinians) was at my wedding. Food is a common element and the one thing most weddings have in common regardless of the religion, culture, location, or socioeconomic status. I know, I know, that seems obvious, but you'd be surprised at some of the responses I get when I mention planning for meals. I even had one potential client who was seriously indignant about having to feed their guests. I decided not to work with her. (Hey, can you blame me?)

The key is to determine what meals/snacks will be provided, the type of food you'd like to have, and how much you are willing to spend per person. But before we jump into the nitty gritty details, let me tell you what to expect.

We will start with hiring a professional and everything you need to know about the hiring process. Then we'll hop to the DIY option. Does that sound good?

Hiring a Professional
Caterers can do far more than just prepare your wedding menu. Not only will they cook and serve the meal, they might even supply the tableware rentals (or rent them for you), help decorate/set the tables,

bake your wedding cake, provide bar services, etc. The level of involvement varies between caterers and can usually be tailored to your needs.

Once you have a short list of caterers, reach out and ask to meet with them. Save yourself some time and use this email template I created for you:

> Hi [Insert Name or Company Name],
>
> I hope you are doing well. [Insert how you heard about them: I was impressed by your catering at an event I attended / a friend recommended you]. I'm reaching out to discuss the possibility of you catering my wedding.
>
> Here are the event details:
> [Month Date, Year] Wedding at [Venue Name, Town, State]. We expect there will be around [Approx. number of people] guests.
>
> I'm looking for a [buffet/sit-down] dinner and [stationed/passed] hor d'ouvres during cocktail hour. We are looking for someone who is able to provide [type of food you desire].
>
> Please let me know if you are available for [wedding date] and if so, an initial quote. If all is good from there, I'd like to set up an in-person meeting to discuss details further.
>
> Talk with you soon,
> [Your Name & Contact Information]

Consultation:
A few things you should discuss with your caterer include:
- Determine table service. Is the meal going to be buffet style, seated, family style, or passed?
- Set the menu. Does the event call for appetizers, salads, soups, breads, entrees, desserts, snacks, coffee/tea, beverages, and/or bartending needs?
- Arrange a tasting to ensure that you are satisfied with the selections. (You might have to pay for this separately, but sometimes the payment is applied to your balance if you book with them.)
- Detail any food allergies or sensitivities of the attendees (allergies, diabetic, vegetarian, special diets, etc.).

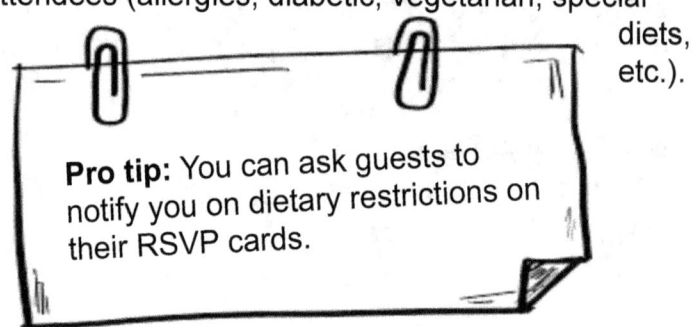

Pro tip: You can ask guests to notify you on dietary restrictions on their RSVP cards.

- Discuss what type of place setting (plates/silverware/glassware) you wish to use. Is it paper, plastic, eco-friendly materials, or fine china? Will you need to rent, borrow, or buy the serveware?
- Determine needs for serving food, including chafing dishes and serving equipment. Will those be provided by the caterer, client or venue?
- Determine the delivery times, set-up requirements, staffing needs, and serving the meal.

Want some more detailed questions? Peruse the list of questions on the next page.

Questions to Ask:
- Are you licensed and insured?
- Can your caterer provide references from previous clients?
- Are you working any other weddings or events on the same weekend or same day? If so, what is the maximum number of weddings you take on each day?
- Do you specialize in certain types of food, such as organic, locally sourced, ethnic or gluten-free? Do you work with fresh, not frozen, food?
- Do you offer full service? Or just cook and deliver?
- Do you have set menu packages? Completely custom menus? What's the average price range for these options?
- When do you need to know the finalized menu choices? How about the final head count?
- Are you able to prepare vegetarian, gluten-free, kosher or halal meals if guests need it? Is there an additional fee for these meals?
- Do you provide vendor meals as part of the package? Or are they at a discounted price? When do you need the vendor headcount by?
- Do you offer kids' meals? Are they the same price?
- Can we arrange a tasting prior to signing a contract? If so, when is that possible? Is if complimentary or is there a fee? How much does it cost?
- Do you also provide cakes and/or bar services?
- Will you provide tables, chairs, plates, napkins, silverware, and salt and pepper shakers? Are they extra? If not, can you rent them for us?

- Do you provide a waitstaff? How many are included in the package? If necessary, what is the fee for additional waitstaff?
- What will the staff wear? May you see photos?
- How do delivery, setup and breakdown work? Is there an additional fee for this? How much time is needed to set up? What time do you/your staff need access to the wedding venue?
- Where will you prepare the food? Will you work in the venue's on-site facilities (if available)? Or will you cook it ahead off site and store it in warming racks until time?
- Will you set out the wedding place cards and menus we created?
- Who will oversee catering on our wedding day? Will it be the same person we work with while planning? Will it be another member of the staff?
- What will happen if the appointed person is sick or otherwise unable to be there? Do you provide a suitable replacement? What is the backup plan?
- Are there any extra charges we should plan for? For example, a security deposit, sales tax, service fees, etc.? What are the expected gratuities?
- How do you arrange the food? May you see photos of previous presentation examples?

Tastings

A tasting can be exploratory (to help you determine the direction you want to go to) and/or after you've decided on a sample menu. It depends on you and your caterer. Either one is considered standard. (I almost used the word normal... ick. Normal is boring).

Helpful Reminder: Come Hungry!

Contracts
Once you'd decided on one caterer, ask to see a sample contract. Know all the terms before you sign. Established catering providers tend to have a standardized contract. The contract typically includes the date, times, location, services required, and payment terms. If you find that the service provider does not have a contract template, create a document with all the pertinent details and have everyone involved sign and date the agreement.

Doing it Yourself
Don't want to work with a caterer? No worries! DIY it. You can do this by preparing things yourself, purchasing food from a grocery store/discount store, having family/friends help, etc. Here are some things to consider:

Preparing it Yourself
This is a great option to help save money. Some people create large patches of food ahead and freeze them. Others try to cook/prepare everything that day or the day before. Something to consider: this option might come with some added stress. You'll already be running around doing 500 last minute things - half of which you weren't expecting. They might cut into cooking time.

Having Friends/Family Help
Don't want to do all the cooking yourself? Ask for help! Enlist your family and friends to prepare the meal. They can be in charge of one particular dish. Or you can involve all your guests. Ask for people to bring a dish to share instead of a gift. Potluck

weddings can promote a warm atmosphere and close-knit-community feel.

Purchasing Food
You can buy large amounts of hor d'oeuvres from the grocery store or full casseroles from your favorite large discount store (Costco, Sam's Club, etc.). Or you can order platters from the store's deli/catering service. You order it and set it up at the venue yourself. You can do something similar to this with a number of fast food chains and full-service restaurants. Shop around for the best prices.

Delegating Catering Duty
If you plan to DIY the food, it is advisable that you delegate those duties to specific family and friends. Don't leave it to chance. Make sure people know they are responsible for picking up the food, storing it, setting it up, monitoring supply during the night, and cleaning up. The last thing you want is to be moving a large tray of spaghetti in your nice clothes.

Determining Food Amounts
If you are DIYing this portion, you'll need to know how to determine the amount of food you need to make and/or buy.

Determining Food Amounts
How Much Do You Really Need?

Industry standards suggest 1 plate of food per person, plus 30% extra of each course.

Serving Sizes:

6oz. of 1 main dish (Poultry, Meat or Fish)
or 8oz. if two or more main courses

1.5oz. of Rice or Grains if side dish or
2oz. If part of main dish (i.e. risotto)

2 oz. of Pasta as a side dish
Or 3 oz. if as first course
Or 4oz. If as main course

5 oz. Potatoes
4 oz. Vegetable
2 oz. Beans as a side dish
1 oz. Green Salad (undressed weight)
4 oz. Soup

Things to Keep in mind:

- Teens eat 1.5 x 2 times as much as an older adult
- The more dishes on the menu, the less of each is needed.
- Plan at least one vegetarian entree
- Expect to accommodate people's dietary restrictions (plan to ask for these during the RSVP process).

 Flowers have been strongly linked to weddings for years. Most couples involve flowers in some form or fashion. However, many people don't realize how expensive they are until they start talking with florists. Be prepared to have sticker shock.

Also be prepared for the "upsell." I've witnessed and been told about florists who are upselling ninjas. By that I mean they can flawlessly upsell more expensive ideas by kindly dismissing every idea the customer offers. It doesn't matter how great the customer's ideas are, they know how to get more money out of the deal. It is seamless and most people never realize what is happening. The florist usually comes away with at least a few hundred dollars more than if they'd stuck with the customer's original ideas. I have no idea how they do it, but I've seen it time and time again.

To help you combat this type of upselling sorcery, **try the following tips:**

- Figure out what flowers are going to be in season at the time of your wedding before you talk with the florist. These will be the cheaper options.
- Pick three to five florists and interview them. It'll give you enough information to determine what your options are without getting overwhelmed by the amount of information they'll give you.

- When you first visit a potential florist, don't tell them anything about you (no ideas, no budget). Even though you've already decided that information, keep it to yourself during the first meeting. It'll prevent the florist from immediately playing games. Plus, you'll get more honest answers this way.
- Ask them LOTS of questions during the first meeting. See the list below for some ideas.
- Have a fairly solid idea of blooms and styles you want. Don't be talked down unless the reason is completely legit (example: the type of flowers you want are only grown out of the country and would need to be flown in the day before and your wedding is nowhere near a major airport).
- Ask for their portfolio and make sure they are real photos of actual events that the florist did themselves. Don't accept stock photos or standardized books. Make sure it is their own work.
- Out-of-season flowers can be super expensive. Yes, your florist can probably get them for you, but they might be five times more expensive than when it is in season.
- Don't haggle. There are industry standards that dictate pricing. Haggling will just put the florist in a bad mood, and he/she might look for ways to upcharge you.
- Ask about the potentially hidden charges. Things like delivery fees, set-up fees, or paying for travel.
- Do not bug your florist. Limit your calls, emails and certainly don't "just drop by."

Questions to Ask
- How many weddings do you do each weekend? Do you have a maximum number? How many are currently on my date?
- What are your stylistic mainstays? Can I see examples?
- Can you show me an example of what you did for another _____ (insert: location, theme, time of year, etc.) wedding before?

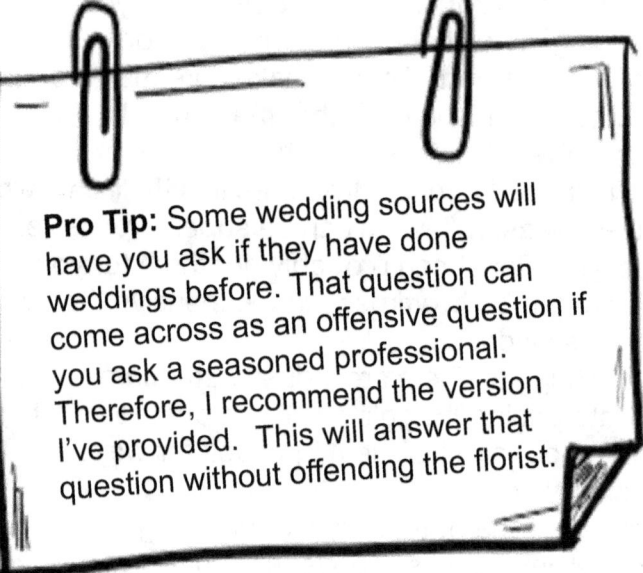

Pro Tip: Some wedding sources will have you ask if they have done weddings before. That question can come across as an offensive question if you ask a seasoned professional. Therefore, I recommend the version I've provided. This will answer that question without offending the florist.

- Do you have additional photos of previous work? May I review them?

Pro Tip: Check their website for examples BEFORE talking with them. Chances are you'll be able to determine if you like their style from the website and won't have to ask this.

- What is the typical budget you work with?
- Can you realistically work within my budget? If so, what would that look like?
- What does the price include?
- Will you be arranging my flowers or will another member of the staff be in charge of this?
- If a flower arrives damaged or unavailable for my event, will you notify me before you substitute it? Or do you reserve the right to substitute it without my consent?
- Can I rent display items (vases, pedestals, etc.) from you? If so, what do you have available?
- What is your delivery fee?
- Who would deliver the flowers and when? (morning of, night before, etc.)
- What are your insurance, cancellation and refund policies?
- What are your general terms of contract? Could I see a sample contract?

DIY:
This section will be about DIY live flowers. See the Alternatives to Live Flowers Section for other options.

Flowers can be one of the largest expenses for weddings. A potentially cheaper option is doing the flowers yourself.

But don't go into this thinking it'll be easy. You can't just throw some stems together and call it a bouquet… Okay, you can… but just don't expect it to look like a professional did it (unless you are a professional florist; then ignore this).

Remember that florists train for years and could do this in their sleep. That said, if you're creative and willing, you can achieve a suitable substitute.

When planning to DIY live flowers, consider the following:
- Stroll around your local farmers' market. Talk with growers who sell cut flowers.
- Look online at wholesalers and figure out how flowers are shipped. Are there ordering limits (i.e. an entire case of 100 flowers)?
- Determine if there is a local flower wholesaler in the area and if they allow people outside the industry to purchase from them.
- If you are looking for petals, don't pay extra for them! Pick up a bouquet at the supermarket and destroy it yourself. There is no need to pay someone else to take apart a bloom.
- Check with your local discount stores and supermarkets to see if you can get a discount ordering in bulk.

Remember that wherever you get your flowers from, you'll need to have them fresh for the day of your wedding. That might mean cutting/picking up the flowers that morning and arranging them before you start getting ready in the morning.

You can also arrange them the night before. The key is to have a refrigerated space in which to store them. This is the option I chose for my own wedding. I picked up the flowers from the wholesaler the morning before my wedding. I then arranged the table flowers that afternoon and stored them in the venue's refrigerated space overnight.

Once you have the flowers in your possession, you'll have to arrange them. If you are looking for flower arranging tutorials, search youtube. You can find all kinds of helpful tutorials online.

Alternatives to Live Flowers:
Nothing says that you have to have live flowers at your wedding. Silk flowers, paper flowers, and non-florals are routinely used in lieu of living flowers.

Silk Flowers
A lot of couples immediately think that going with silk flowers will save them money. Unfortunately, that isn't actually the case. Silk Flowers can be just as expensive. What it will do is provide you with plenty of time to design your own bouquets and centerpieces. You can create them months in advance and not worry about them wilting.

To find silk flowers, I recommend starting at your local arts and crafts store. They will have a decent selection and will let you see what you like in person. Price things out there. Then go online and see what options you can find there. You'll likely find options for buying single stems, in bulk, prearranged, etc.

Paper Flowers
Another trend I've seen is paper flowers. They can be made using tissue paper, origami, or thicker craft paper. Some people make one large tissue paper bloom while others create an entire mixed bouquet of paper flowers.

Forget the Flowers
Want to forgo the flowers altogether? No problem. Try one of these options:

- Fans (excellent for hot outdoor weddings)
- Bouquets made out of alternative materials (yarn, buttons, found objects, etc.)

- Paper-based flowers, pinwheels, origami cranes, etc.
- Animals (I've heard of bridesmaids carrying bunnies, puppies, etc. Just be sure they don't pee on you as you are carrying them; try walking them on leashes instead).
- Balloons (make sure none of your guests are war veterans; popping balloons can sometimes trigger PTSD responses)
- Centerpieces out of books, lanterns, candles, mirrors, picture frames, etc.
- Edible bouquets (cotton candy, fruit, vegetables ... heck, I've even heard of pizza bouquets. My only word of warning — don't eat them before the ceremony)

Anything goes. It's your wedding.

Music

Musicians/DJ/Bands
There are many different music options for you and your wedding. This section will walk you through a few different common options. We will start with DJs, move on to Bands, and discuss DIY options.

Storytime...

> I worked one wedding where the DJ had it rough. The wedding was in a poor, rural area. The bride and groom were lovely, but some of their family members were a bit rough around the edges.
>
> Okay… I was trying to be polite… they were rednecks who probably hadn't been sober in years. I promise, I have nothing against rednecks. I grew up in a small Southern town with a working barn on the high school campus. I'm just trying to give you a visual.
>
> Back to the story. The bride's cousin was wasted by the time the DJ started playing his set (around 8 pm). She went up to the DJ almost every three minutes. It started out okay, but as time goes by I could see him getting…

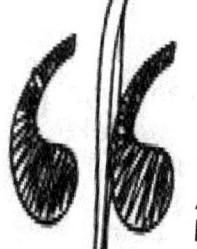

"... visibly annoyed and her getting increasingly belligerent.

I later found out that those conversations were her requesting to make a "toast". Apparently the bride suspected that might happen because she had basically told the DJ early in the night to refuse to let her cousin speak. This instruction didn't help him deal with the reality.

The more he refused to give her the microphone, the more the cousin freaked out. She finally started screaming and trying to steal the microphone from him.

None of the guests seemed all that surprised. Eventually, another family member physically removed her from the room.

So the moral of the story, prep your DJ. If he hadn't been told about the potential issue, he might have given the cousin the microphone."

...Storytime

DJs
You can help prepare you DJ in a few ways.

Questionnaires
They ask you to fill out a music selection questionnaire. You can tell them you don't want them to accept requests. Also have a do-not-play list. Make sure you get those to your DJ in plenty of time (by their deadline). It'll be worth it.

Decide on Talking Level
Do you want a silent person behind the turntables? Or a sports commentator engaging the room?

To help you find a good match, research the DJs available in your area. Then reach out to your top 3-5 choices. You can use the following email to help things get rolling.

> Hi [Insert DJ Name or Company Name],
>
> I hope you are doing well. I read about your DJ services for weddings and I'm interested in getting a quote for my wedding.
>
> Here are the event details:
> [Month Date, Year] Wedding at [Venue Name, Town, State]. There will be approximately [#] guests.
>
> I'm looking for DJ services during the reception for [number of hours]. We are looking for someone who [will engage the crowd regularly / keep talking to a minimum / announce the important moments] throughout the night.

> Please let me know if you are available for [Wedding Date]. If so, I would love an initial quote. If all is good from there, I'd like to set up an in person meeting to discuss details further.
>
> I hope to talk with you soon,
> [Your Name & Contact Information]

Backup plan
Once you find someone who fits your needs, ask them about the worst case scenario. What happens if they are sick or can't be there? Do they have someone already in line to cover them? Are they part of a company that has numerous DJs on staff who can fill in if need be? Figure out the details and have them included in the contract.

Bands
Bands are an excellent option for wedding entertainment. As with any musician act, there are a few points to consider before booking them.

- Determine what range of music they play. If they are a swing band, they probably won't be prepared to cover a hip hop track.
- Have you heard them play before? Do they have tracks you can listen to? Videos of them performing? Make sure you like their sound before you book.

- Remember that they will only be able to play for a set amount of time before they'll need to take a break. Make sure you are prepared to accommodate this.

Have the information you need and you are ready to move forward? Try using the following email template for contacting bands:

> Hi [Insert Name or Band Name],
>
> I hope you are doing well. [Insert how you heard about them.] I'm interested in discussing the possibility of you playing at my wedding.
>
> Here are the event details:
>
> [Month Date, Year] Wedding at [Venue Name, Town, State].
>
> I'm looking for you all to play during the reception for [number of hours]. We are looking for someone who is able to play [type of music you desire].
>
> Please let me know if you are available for [Wedding Date] and if so, an initial quote. If all is good from there, I'd like to set up an in person meeting to discuss details further.
>
> I look forward to hearing from you,
>
> [Your Name & Contact Information]

Musicians

As I've mentioned before, people love to tell me (as an event planner) their wedding horror stories. There are two stories I want to share about musicians.

> Someone told me once about how they hired a harp player who ended up being 9 months pregnant on the wedding date. Her water broke not even half an hour after the ceremony was over. She was just about to leave the church parking lot. It was a close call. And this has motivated the couple to encourage everyone they know to have a backup plan.

Storytime...

> I worked an event where the band was later banned from that venue. They performed their set as planned without any snafus. However, the lead singer snuck off at the end of the night with one of my co-workers. They were found by security an hour later allegedly hooking up and smoking pot. The rest of the staff was told that the band wasn't allowed to perform there anymore and the employee had been terminated. Moral of the story: make sure you get references for your musician. Get references from the clients and the venues if you can manage it.

Not sure where to find upstanding musicians who have talent, integrity, and a solid back-up plan? Try these avenues:

Hiring Ceremony Musicians:
Does the place of worship have regular musicians? If so, do they do weddings too? Musicians who play for a place of worship routinely have a few things going for them: 1) they have a long-standing relationship with that community and won't risk messing it up during your wedding; 2) they know the instruments and/or equipment set-up well; 3) they likely have a back-up plan and someone they call if they can't make a gig.

Hiring Reception Musicians:
Start by asking the venue coordinator if they have a list of preferred musicians. These people will have an established relationship with the venue and will have proven themselves respectable. If not, search for local musicians and ask for references.

Once you've found potential musicians, reach out them. Consider using the following email template:

Hi [Insert Name],

I hope you are doing well. [Insert how you heard about them: I heard you play at location / a friend recommended you]. I'm interested in discussing the possibility of you playing at my wedding.

Here are the event details: [Month Date, Year] Wedding at [Venue Name, Town, State].

I'm looking for you to play during the [ceremony/reception] for [number of hours]. We are looking for something who is able to play [type of music].

Please let me know if you are available for [Date] and if so, an initial quote. If all is good from there, I'd like to set up a meeting to discuss details further.

Talk with you soon,
[Your Name & Contact Information]

Questions to Ask
Once you make contact with the musicians, find out the answers to the following questions:

- Are they going to be solo during the reception?
- Are they working with other musicians?
- Have they worked with the other musicians before? If so, how often? If not, are they comfortable with playing with other musicians?
- Are they going to be there the entire reception? Or are they playing during a specific part (dinner, cocktail hour, etc.)?
- What do they plan to do if they are sick or break a hand and can't play? Do they have a back-up person they can call?

Your Own Sound System:
It is tempting to forgo the price of a professional band and/or DJ. If you can afford it, it's worth it. If you can't or don't want to, you can use your own system.

Storytime...

One wedding I was working involved someone hooking up their phone to the house sound system. It was a nightmare. First, we couldn't plug it in. The built-in connectors of the system were a few years old. The bride had updated to the newest iPhone AFTER our tech-run-through (aka our test run)... with a different jack than the system had. We tried every toggle we could find; nothing worked. My assistant had to run out to Best Buy to get the correct adapter.

Once we got it plugged in and working (part way through dinner), it kept lagging between songs because they were streaming (not downloaded). The internet speed usually isn't an issue at this venue, but someone in the wedding party gave out the login information to the majority of the guests. So many people were on the wifi that it slowed down the 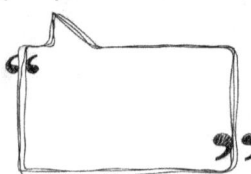 system. The worst part of it all? During the couples' first dance, someone called her and her ringtone was highly inappropriate.

How to avoid issues when using your own music:
- Make sure you've tested the system with all the equipment you are going to use.

- Have at least 2-3 backup options. That can be playlists loaded on other people's phones, a laptop with the information, saved to the cloud, a USB drive, hell, even a recorded CD. Make sure you have options in case something stops working.
- Have the playlist downloaded onto your device. Yeah, it'll take up a lot of memory, but it's best to have the option. Relying on streaming is tricky; it isn't always the best quality.

Tech Run-Throughs
Always do a tech run-through. This means testing the exact equipment you are going to use during the wedding. These test runs usually occur a few days before the event. The goal is to ensure everything works correctly the day of the wedding. If you discover an issue, you have plenty of time to fix it. If the tech run goes smoothly, it will give everyone peace of mind.

Back-up Plans
It doesn't matter which option you choose… always have a back up plan. Be a Girl Scout; be prepared! (any other scouts out there?)

AV System
Regardless of the route you choose to go, you are going to need to pay attention to the audio visual (AV) requirements. The easiest way is to ask the venue coordinator if they have a technical specifications document (casually referred to "tech specs" by some). It may seem like Greek to you, but it is necessary to find out.

Audio Visual Requirements
The type of event will determine the audio visual requirements. For example, bands will need extensive sound equipment; presentations will need projectors, microphones, and computers; and simple parties might only need a stereo.

A helpful way to determine the audio visual needs is to run through a checklist. Ask your venue coordinator, your vendor, and yourself, if the event will require the following:

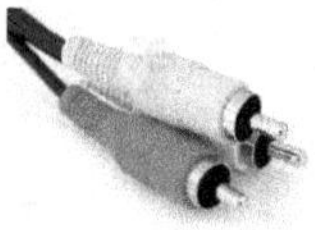

- Projector
- Computer
- Sound system
- Handheld Microphone
- Microphone stands
- Podium with Microphone
- Stereo equipment
- Sound Board
- DVD/VHS player
- TV
- Speakers
- Laser Pointer
- Remote presentation mouse
- Wired internet connection
- Wireless internet connection

 Choosing an officiant is a very personal choice. That's why I've broken down this section into types of officiants, how to find an officiant, and things to keep in mind. You can pick the section that most applies to you and your partner's wishes.

Religious Ceremonies
If you and/or your partner is a member of a religious organization, you may already have a religious officiant in mind. Or if you are getting married in a house of worship, there may be an officiant responsible for that location. This means it would be relatively easy to find a priest, rabbi, vicar, minister, imam, or other religious officiant to marry you. Keep in mind this will likely mean a traditional ceremony.

Interfaith Ceremonies
I've been involved with a number of interfaith ceremonies. Some will have officiants from both religions while others will have a secular officiant customize the ceremony. For example, my college friends had both a Catholic priest and a rabbi perform a joint ceremony.

If you are looking for pastors, priests, ministers, rabbis, imam, and/or other religious officiants who are open to performing interfaith ceremonies, try your local university or college. They are typically used to working with a diverse community and can be more open to performing interfaith ceremonies.

Civil Ceremonies
If you and your partner are not religious and/or want a secular ceremony, you can look for celebrants, secular officiants, judges, civil servant, justices of the peace, or ask family/friends. The professional officiants will likely be certified by an organization or the local government. If you go the friends/family route, you'll need to make sure they are legally allowed to marry you. This can be done online, through the state, etc.

Make sure your officiant is ordained according to the laws of the state in which the wedding takes place. Some states will push back against people ordained online while others will provide a special pass for a day. For example, in Vermont you can apply to the state and ask for permission to marry a specific couple on a specific day. My husband went through this process and married our friends one fall. In North Carolina, they might call the validity of your marriage into question if you used someone who was ordained online.

Regardless of who you choose and where you get married, it is important that you check local laws and ensure your officiant meets all the requirements. Make sure you are following the rules.

Finding an officiant
How you choose your officiant will vary depending on your faith tradition and your location. Here are a few common ways of finding an officiant:

- Speak with your own house of worship to see if the main religious celebrant is available

- Check out the local houses of worship for additional options
- Look into the religious officiants at the local university or college
- Call the town/city/county/state offices to ask about local justices of the peace
- See if your venue or event planner has a list of recommendations
- Ask your family/friends if they know of anyone or even ask them to officiate your wedding

Check the Local Laws
Make sure your officiant is ordained according the laws of the state in which the wedding takes place. Some states will push back against people ordained online while others will provide a special pass for a day. Regardless of which state you are getting married in, it is important that you check local laws and ensure your officiant meets all the requirements.

Marriage License
Regardless of who your officiant will be, you will need to apply for the marriage license. Check your state and town for local requirements. Your officiant will fill it out and witness your signatures. Most of the times, the officiant will mail the paperwork back for you. However, there are cases where you will return the license on your own. Ask your officiant the way they normally handle this so you aren't surprised.

Determine if you need to apply for the marriage license with your town of residence or the town you are getting married in. They can have different requirements.

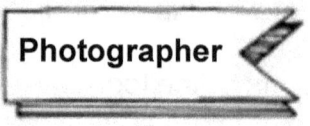 As an event planner, people like to tell me their wedding stories. The one that breaks my heart the most is hearing about the couples who hate their wedding photos.

I can't solve their problem after the fact, but I can offer advice to help you avoid the pain of wedding photo regret. I'll walk you through the best way to hire the right photographer for you, questions you actually want to know the answers to, and how to make your photographer's life easier (i.e., help them get better photos of you).

How to Hire The Right Photographer:
First off, let's talk about hiring a photographer that is right for you. It's not going to be the same for everyone, but I can give you the process of finding the best person for you to work with.

1. Jive with their Style
So, how do you pick a photographer? First, do some research. Look through their websites and find ones who have photos that appeal to your style.

Every photographer has a different approach. You found one photographer whose images look sharp and clean, one whose images are soft and pastel, some who specialize in blurry backgrounds, and another person who has a vintage look. It doesn't matter which look you go with, as long as you like it.

Once you've shortlisted your favorite photographers, reach out and set up a time to meet them. (Save yourself time and use the email template at the end of this section.)

Pro Tip: Make sure you meet with the photographer, not a sales consultant or studio owner. There are such things as wedding photography mills where you talk with a sales person and then are sent an inexperienced, underpaid photographer the day of your wedding. Be sure you meet with the person who will be with you on your wedding.

2. Like your photographer (as a person)

You should like them, not only their images. Be sure you are comfortable around them and enjoy your photographer as a person. You'll be spending a lot of time with them. They will be following you around all day. You need to know, like and trust them for your own sake.

Pro Tip: Want to know if you'll like your photographer? Meet them in person. Have your consultation at a local coffee shop. During the meeting, chat a bit before you jump into business. Is this someone you would get coffee with again as friends? Your answer will help you decide.

3. Tread cautiously when hiring friends or family

It can be dangerous to mix business with pleasure. Best case scenario: photographer friends/friends offer to take your photos out of kindness, but then they can't be guests at your wedding. They are working all night. Worst case scenario: you don't like their work and/or they are terrible to do business with, things escalate, and your personal relationship is ruined. Okay, it might not ruin your relationship, but weddings bring out the worst in people so asking your family/friends to work for you will certainly strain your relationship.

I whole-heartedly recommend allowing your family and friends to be guests at your wedding. I'll let you in on a secret: wedding photographers never get to be guests. They'll appreciate the break. It's refreshing to attend a wedding where they can leave the camera at home, have a drink, and hit the dance floor.

4. Choose a professional WEDDING photographer

Hire a professional. Experience means they will be able to capture all the special moments with skill. Also, hire someone who specializes in weddings and has shot a lot of them. Just because someone is an amazing food photographer, it doesn't mean that person can document a wedding. It is a different set of skills.

5. Book an engagement session

Not sure if you really want to work with someone? Book an engagement session. That way you can "test drive" the photographer before the big day. If you've already decided on a photographer, you should still absolutely do an engagement photo session, especially if it is already included. The engagement will get you familiar with the photographer's working style and what their photos look like.

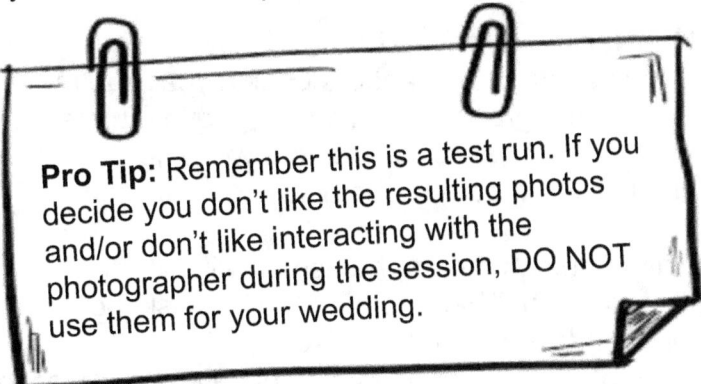

Pro Tip: Remember this is a test run. If you decide you don't like the resulting photos and/or don't like interacting with the photographer during the session, DO NOT use them for your wedding.

Questions You Actually Want to Ask
Most wedding books will give you a list of boring questions to ask a wedding photographer. I read through those and think no one actually cares about all this. It's pointless stuff like: "What equipment do you shoot with?"

Really? Do you really care what camera they are working with? Unless you are a professional photographer yourself, you probably won't have any idea what it means. Plus, the quality of camera is only part of it.

Or my personal favorite: "Can you describe your style?" Ummm... do you really want to hear them verbalize their artistic style or do you want to see it? Even if they've developed a kickass response to that question, their photos will be able give you a more accurate answer.

Let's be real: those questions are boring. So let's talk about the questions you really want to ask.

1. How far in advance should I book?
Many wedding photographers book a year out. In-demand photographers can book out even further than that. As it gets closer to your wedding date, it will be harder to book a photographer.

If your favorite photographer isn't available, don't panic too much. That happened to me. Ask them for recommendations! They've likely worked with a number of second shooters who have a very styles to them. If not, they likely know someone with a similar style and a lighter schedule.

This is actually what happened to me for my own wedding. I'd known which photographer I wanted long before I even got engaged. They were a dream to work with and produced amazing photos. When I contacted them more than a year in advance, they already had a personal commitment on that weekend. They suggested I reach out to one of their second shooters and gave me her contact information. Below is the actual email I wrote to my photographer:

> Hi Katie Jean,
>
> I heard about you through *another photographer*. They recommended I check out your portfolio and I love your work! It is just the creative, candid style Carl and I are looking for.
>
> So I figure you probably want to know a little about our wedding, so here are the basics: We are getting

> married on *date* in *town, state*. The ceremony will be held at *location* and the reception is at *location*. Carl and I met in *town* and we lived near *reception location* for a few years. The picturesque views and the fun we had there made us think it would be fitting to have our wedding there.
>
> I'd love to grab a cup of coffee to chat about what you do and what we are hoping for in a photographer (creative, loves what they do, and most of all lets us be the silly couple we are). I look forward to talking with you and seeing if we are a good fit.
>
> Best,
> Samantha

Please note that I removed personal information for privacy reasons.

2. Why is wedding photography so expensive?

This is a question I see a lot. Wedding photography seems like it should be cheap — photographers work for one day, right? Nope. Full-time wedding photographers often work 60-hour weeks. They work weddings on the weekend and then spend all week editing all the photos. It can take a full week of work to go through and edit the 1,000 photos they took.

Then add on the extra costs of equipment. Wedding photographers can carry over $10,000 in gear. They also have to pay for insurance, office/studio space, software, taxes, advertising, business expenses, etc.

I tell you all this to let you know that while it seems like you are paying them a lot of money, they are likely making less than minimum wage.

3. Do I really need a second photographer?
Okay, you might not *need* one... BUT a second shooter will provide you with more images and a different perspective. They also provide some basic insurance against memory card failure. Even a great photographer who does everything right can have a technical failure. Having a second photographer with them means you've got a whole other set of images on different sets of memory cards and different cameras. Most photographers have someone they work with on a regular basis and will contact directly. You only deal with the head photographer when discussing options.

If your photographer prefers to work solo or if you decide you don't want a second photographer, ask your photographer if they shoot with two different cameras. What this means is that they have two different camera bodies and they switch off between to two. This insures there are two camera and two memory cards. It'll make it so they readily have a backup.

4. Is "shoot and burn" photography a good deal?
Generally, no. It is not a good deal. "Shoot and burn" is slang for photographing a wedding and providing the digital files without any post-processing.

It's usually super cheap but it comes with a cost. Shoot and burn provides you with all of those terrible photos too — the closed eyes, weird faces, bad lighting, photobombers, blemishes, etc.

Unless you are a professional photographer and have years of photoshop experience, getting raw photos isn't the best idea. A full-service photographer will remove all the duds, edit the images, and provide a few proofs before sending you a full portfolio.

5. What is a "first look" and do I need it?

I've seen it before, the photographer asks a couple if they are doing a first look and they are met with blank stares. A first look is when couples see each other privately before the ceremony. If you are a traditionalist and think it's bad luck to see each other, then don't do this. If you don't care or believe in that, then doing a first look will help your photographer out. It will give you a dedicated time to do couple portraits prior to the hectic pace of the ceremony and reception. An added bonus is that it'll help the couple avoid some stress. You can get out the pre-ceremony jitters by having some alone time together and it'll allow you time to mingle with your guests at cocktail hour. (Side note: cocktail hour is the other common time photos happen).

6. How do I make sure I look good in the photos?

Relax. If you're relaxed, it'll come through in your photos. I recommend leaving some breathing room in your schedule so you don't feel rushed. See the section on day-of timelines for tips on how to build in extra time.

Oh, and take it easy at the rehearsal dinner. Wedding-day hangovers are no fun and make you look terrible. Instead, stay hydrated and get plenty of sleep the night before.

7. How many photos do I get?

The average is 50-100 photos for every hour of coverage. If your ceremony is an hour, you get 50 - 100 photos of that. If your photographer stays for 4 hours of the reception, there are another 200-400 photos. Hundreds of photos may seem like a lot, but your wedding photographer is making sure to capture all those important moments as well as all those guest interactions you might have missed.

8. Can I see the entire set of photographs?

The smartest question a potential client can ask is: "may I see the ENTIRE set of photographs you provided to a couple? I'd like to see all of them, not just the ones in your portfolio." By seeing an entire collection of photos you'll get a much better sense of what you will receive.

Help Out and Give Your Photographer a Break....

You've hired a photographer you like personally and who meets your style requirements. Now it is time to help them get the best possible photos. Below are a few stress-inducing pet peeves and precautionary fixes. So help your photographer out...

1. Timing

Snafus don't just stress out the couple and the event planner, they also impact your photographer. Ambitious timelines, unexpected traffic delays, hair and makeup running late, impromptu snack break — can all take away from your photo time. So please pad your timeline! (See page 183 for help with this) Your day will feel much more relaxed and you'll get more photos.

2. Must-have photo lists
Nothing pisses off your photographer more than providing a "must-have" photo list, especially one that is clearly printed off the internet and starts with something like "Bride looking over shoulder." Really? Really? Come on!

Professional photographers want to capture things that are important to you and give you photos you love. However, a long list of basic imagery can stifle creativity and make your photographer miss things because they're too busy working through your list.

A better plan is to communicate what is most important to you: Details? Real moments? Photos of the guests? Who are the most important people to you? Then let them work their magic. That's what you hired them to do.

3. Don't be a Pinterest-stalker
Pinterest can be a wonderful tool, but it can also be the enemy. Don't expect your photography to recreate everything on your latest board. A photographer never wants to copy someone else's work. It is the artistic version of stealing.

Plus, you don't know the story behind each of the images, the lighting required to get that effect, what happened to inspire that response, or even if they are a real couple. They could be hired models for stock photography session.

In short, remember that aspiring to copy Pinterest will set you up for disappointment. Do your photographer a favor and don't email them asking "can you do this?" while attaching your Pinterest board.

4. Avoid the Weird Lighting
Nothing is worse than bad lighting. It can ruin the photos and make it extremely difficult for your photographer. The two main culprits: sunlight and laser lights.

Sunlight: Nobody wants squinty eye photos or shadowy images with the one person in the sun and the other in the shade. Figure out where the sun will be at that time and plan accordingly.

Pro Tip: If your ceremony is outside, try to find a spot where the sun will be behind you, hitting your shoulders. For late-morning and early-afternoon weddings, standing in complete shade is ideal.

Laser Lights: Avoid laser lights all together. The DJ might use them to great effect on the dance floor, but your photographer hates them. No one looks good with green spots on their face. No, not even you, you gorgeous thang you.

5. Feed your photographer
I've heard so many debates about if you "have to" feed your vendors. Please do! It is not only the kind thing to do, it'll make everything go so much more smoothly. Be sure to ask your caterer to feed your photographer at the same time they serve you. If you don't plan for a coordinated serve time, the caterer might try to feed the photographer at the exact moment that you are cutting the cake or having your first dance. If your photographer is eating the same time you are, they will have a chance to eat and not miss any important photo ops.

6. Tell People to Behave
Inappropriate guests are a big problem for photographers. There is a disturbing trend of groomsmen exposing themselves to the camera or couples faking sex acts for the camera. Don't be those people. Have some self-respect.

7. Prevent Wardrobe Malfunctions
Speaking of the uncomfortable intersection of inappropriate exposure and photos, can we talk about brides needing to constantly adjust their dress so their boobs don't pop out of it? It makes for some awkward photos. When purchasing a dress consider all the activities you'll be doing during the wedding. Stand, sit, and dance in the fitting room to discover any potential issues. Find a comfortable dress you're not fussing with all day.

After the Wedding Timeline
It'll likely take some time for the photographer to provide you with the final product. Don't expect the images right away. I know you are excited to see them, but editing the end product isn't a quick job.

The average wait time for photos and videos is typically between 2-6 weeks. The time it actually takes will vary depending on the photographer, their schedule, how many photos they took that day, how much editing each photo needs, etc.

 Determine how long it'll take before your wedding and follow up with them when it nears that expected date. It'll be worth the wait. Be patient in the meantime.

Many photographers will try to send you a sneak peak early on and then the finished product at a later date.

If you start feeling frustrated that you haven't gotten back the final product yet, remember that your photographer usually spends much more time editing the images than they do capturing them.

Photographers have to go through thousands of images. They take out the awful shots as well as edit the best photos. Editing including cropping, adjusting the color, removing blemishes, etc. They are working hard to create that finished style you hired them for.

Rental Company

In most areas of the US there is one major rental company that supplies the majority of items for local events and weddings. The one in Vermont is called Vermont Tent Company. It rents almost anything and I mean ANYTHING. It rents the traditional dishes, cloth napkins, tents, tables/chairs, but it also rents dance floors, stages, outdoor heaters, couches, vases, and Greek columns.

Visiting one of these warehouses as an event planner is a bit different from visiting as a bride/groom. As an event planner, you usually do all your business by phone/email and only stop in the back to deliver a forgotten table linen. This means you head to the service entrance. While that might sound degrading, it is actually fascinating. It means I get to see their storage facilities and the sheer number of items they have available. As a bride/groom or potential customer, you have a completely different experience. You are greeted in the posh waiting room and have an in-person consultation with a sales rep who shows you a nicely manicured showroom. It's more like a high-end home goods store than anything else, only everything is for rent.

You'll be asked to make a decision on a number of items. I've listed a few common categories couples should consider.

Portable Bathrooms
Yup, that's right. You can usually find a company that rents portable bathrooms. Having your wedding in a tent without plumbing nearby? At a historic location where the plumbing can't withstand a crowd? You should look into renting bathrooms.

Now I'm not talking about typical porta-potties. You can get those too, but you can class it up if you want. There are entire luxury bathroom trailers with everything from working fireplaces to mahogany trim.

A few things to consider:

Thinking Numbers:
Plan for a least one toilet for every fifty guests. If your wedding is longer than 5 hours, you'll need to plan for additional restrooms.

Battle of the Sexes:
Individual bathrooms are unisex. However, if you go with trailers, you may wish to designate men's & women's. If you do so, be sure you dedicate more toilets to women. It'll help cut down on lines.

Be ADA Compliant:
Be sure that at least one of the bathrooms is handicapped accessible.

Consider Placement:
Put the bathrooms close enough for convenience but also be sure they are far enough away to be discrete. Also be sure to post directional signs and light the path there.

Dance Floor
If you have an indoor venue, it's unlikely that you'll need to rent a dance floor. However, if you have a tent wedding, you'll likely need to rent one. The size of the dance floor should be determined based on your number of guests. The standard is approximately 2.5 square feet per person. The rental company will likely help you with this, but it's nice to know the math behind it all the same.

Furniture (Table/Chair Rentals)
Table and chair availability varies by venue. Some venues will supply and set up all tables and chairs. Others will require that you rent the furniture from an event rental company. When renting furniture, it is important to consider the following:
- Number of guests
- Particular room set-up
- Number of rooms the event will span
- How many tables and chairs are required for each room?
- The needs of the catering/bar company (extra tables for set-up)
- Is the furniture provided by the venue?
- Will the venue provide set-up services?
- Are there extras available for last minute additions?

Chairs
You need to consider seating options for three different portions of your wedding: the ceremony, the cocktail hour, and the reception. Below are a few tips you might want to consider.

Pro Tips

Tip #1: If you are renting chairs for an outdoor ceremony, it is wise to opt for the white plastic folding chairs with a padded seat. This will allow for all weather conditions. If it is hot, they will stay cool. If it is muddy, they are easily cleaned. If it rained earlier that morning, they can be easily dried.

Tip#2 : Cocktail hour does not require seating for everyone. If you have high-top tables, people tend to stand around them. Do provide a few bar stools for those who want to sit.

Tip #3: Be aware of your elderly guests and anyone with mobility issues. It is customary to have standard-height chairs (preferably with backs/arms) provided for them during all portions of the wedding.

Tip#4: If you don't like the chairs the venue provides, you can rent other chairs and/or rent chair covers.

Tip#5: Take note of restrictions. Does your rental company only allow you to have their chairs set up indoors?

Lounge Furniture

If you are looking to create a comfortable, loungelike feel, consider looking into lounge furniture. Some rental companies will rent arm chairs, chaise lounges, couches, ottomans, and large upholstered cushions.

Tables

There are no hard and fast rules about tables and what you can use for your wedding. Since it is so open-ended, I'll give you ideas of what tables to plan for by activity as well as an idea of common table sizes and what they are used for. Work with your venue and the rental company to make sure you are getting what you need and to makes sure it fits in the space.

Common Table Sizes

Size	Use
36in Round	cake display
58-in round	6 to 8 people
60-in round	8 to 10 people
66 in round	10 to 11 people
72 in round	10 to 12 people
48 in square	8 people
60 in square	8 people
72 in square	12 people
8ft Banquet	6 to 8 people
6ft Banquet	4 to 6 people
4 ft Banquet	Gift/Guest Book/Seating Card Table

Tables you should consider

Ceremony
- Guest book table
- Table to hold programs
- Table at the altar

Cocktail Hour
- Guest book table
- Gift Table
- High-tops
- Tables for buffets or food stations
- Tables for the bar

Dinner
- Seating-Card Table
- Head Table
- Sweetheart table
- Cake Table
- Guest Tables (usually round, sometimes banquet)
- Tables for Buffets or food stations

Bar Area:
- High-tops
- Coffee tables
- Food Tables

Tablecloth Linens

It is almost certain that you'll need tablecloths for your cocktail hour and reception. Most of the tables that venues provide and/or that you rent are going to be plastic and greatly benefit from tablecloths. It's traditional to use tablecloths on all tables unless they are a very nice wood deemed "worthy" enough to be shown off.

Tablecloths come in all materials and colors. If you have a color theme, this is one of the places you can match or compliment it.

Length:
Traditional wisdom suggests that you use tablecloths that go all the way to the floor. The reason for this is to hide the table legs. It gives a polished, seamless look to the room.

However, only event planners and detailed-oriented people will notice this. If your venue has tablecloths you can use that extend half-way down and it'll save you a lot of time/stress, then use those. Most people won't notice and those who do probably won't care.

Glossary of Linens

Overlay	an overlay is a decorative cloth that sits on top of the underlay. It usually extends half way down on the sides of the table
Pickup	sometimes the skirt of the table linen is strategically "picked up" and held in place with a decorative touch. Think of how the fabric on some wedding gowns is pinched up to give them some extra volume or decoration.

Runner	table runners are a long strip of fabric that runs the length of the table but don't cover the entire width.
Ruching	This is the pleating around the edge of the table top.
Underlay	This term is used in conjunction with the term overlay. The underlay is the bottom layer. It is a full tablecloth that covers the entire table and falls to the floor.

Napkins
Like linens, you'll have a wide choice of colors and fabrics for napkin rentals. See my short rant about the selection process.

Paper vs. Cloth
Cloth napkins are usually used with dinner. Paper napkins are used for the bar and during cocktail hour. That said, there is nothing saying you have to do that. You could use all paper napkins or all cloth napkins. It's up to you.

Napkin Folding
If you rent cloth napkins, many times your caterer will ask you how you want to fold them. There are more options than just folded and sitting under your flatware. Three common "fancy" folds are the Triangle fold, the Goblet fan fold, and the Pocket fold. *See the images below.*

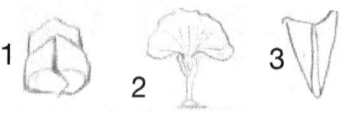

Napkin Folds
1-Pocket, 2-Goblet Fan, 3-Triangle

Storytime...

 Okay, can I just rant for a second? I'm going to assume you said yes. Great, thank you. So, napkins. Yes, you read that right, napkins.

Renting napkins is one of those tasks that makes me want to scream as an event planner. I walk into the posh showroom with a client. The sales rep does her thing talking through options. Then we get to the napkins. And the sales rep always asks "what are your wedding colors?"

I blatantly roll my eyes... don't get me started on wedding colors (that is a rant for later). Even if the couple have chosen wedding colors, they have usually said "blue" and "white." No matter how much prep work I do with a client, they are never truly ready for the color selection process. It is overwhelming.

There are about 10 shades of white and 57 shades of blue. You practically need to know the exact color configuration to even begin to get a close match. Then it moves on to fabric choices. There are not as many options with that one, but it still feels ridiculous.

While the number of choices is overwhelming enough, the pressure the sales rep puts on you is mind-blowing. You'd think that choosing napkin colors and fabrics were the answer to world peace. It is high pressure. Heaven forbid you admit that you don't care! They act like you are an alien. They nearly fall over in shock. One time I said, "no one will remember the napkin color; what is your cheapest option?"

The moral of this story... errr... rant... the rental company's sales rep might act like the decisions you make there are of the utmost importance, but they aren't. It won't ruin your wedding day if you get the "wrong" colored napkins.

Seriously, they are just napkins.

Place settings
If you end up needing to rent china, glassware, flatware, and serving dishes, you'll likely want your caterer's input. They can advise you on the type of things needed, how many, etc. You'll get to decide on the style and cost point. To help you with your decisions, I've included some helpful information below:

China
You can choose from a multitude of plate/bowl options: round, square, basic white plates, something with a gold/silver edge decoration, brightly colored, or uniquely shaped.

Disposable Options: Some people prefer to use disposable plates for easy cleanup. If you are going that direction, opt for a sturdy plate. It can be paper, plastic, or even bamboo.

Glasses
When renting glasses, you'll have to consider the cocktail hour, dinner, and the reception bar. That means you'll need to work with the bar service and the caterer (if they are different) to know how many glasses to order. You'll also need to decide on glassware depending on what drinks you are serving. Think water goblets, champagne flutes, wine glasses, beer glasses, and any speciality bar glasses (margarita, martini, collins, whiskey, etc. all have glasses specific to that drink).

Disposable Options: Some people prefer to use disposable cups and glasses for easy cleanup. If you are going that direction, opt for a sturdy cup. Plastic wine glasses can easy lose their base and certain plastics can crack. There are some great compostable options, too, if you want to got that route.

Silverware
Talk with your caterer to see what each dish will require in terms of utensils. They'll be able to help with the things above and beyond the normal fork, knife, and spoon. It's butter knives, salad forks, soup spoons, steak knives, coffee spoons, etc. You'll also have to decide on utensils for cocktail hour, dinner, and dessert. You'll likely need to have enough for each individual event because there won't be any time to wash the dishes in between and people rarely save their silverware in between courses.

Disposable Options: disposable silverware can be used for easy cleanup. There are plastic, compostable, and even bamboo options. It's up to you.

Serveware
Depending on what type of dinner service you choose, you may also need to rent serving dishes and utensils. This can be chafing dishes, trays, 3-tier displays, serving spoons, cake stands, etc.

Pro Tip: Decide Before you Go

Have you ever gotten the diet advice to look at the menu online and decide on what you are getting before you get to the restaurant? It is supposed to help you stick to your diet and not splurge on some deliciously fried monstrosity that will blow your diet.

Well, my advice for renting place setting is similar. My advice is to look through the company's catalog off-site first and decide on the general style/price point before you visit the showroom. That way you can see all the pieces together in person.

Your caterer will be able to tell you how much extra you need of each thing. Know you have 120 guests? Don't just rent 120 of something. You'll need extras and backups. You'll never know if a plate comes in chipped or a fork gets dropped in the rush. Plan for needing extras.

Pro Tip: Order Extra

Props
You can also rent props and decorations. Think: vases, chandeliers, statues and columns. Ask for the catalog and see if anything would work for your decor.

Stage
If you plan to have a band, they might need a stage. Check with them about requirements. They will usually have size requirements in mind. If for some reason they don't, the rental company can help you determine the required height and total square footage.

Tents
Many brides start out thinking they'll save money by just putting up a tent in an outdoor location. That is not usually the case. It's actually quite expensive. Here are a few things you should consider:

Permits
Depending on your location, some towns/locations will require a permit to allow you to put up a tent. The

rental company and/or venue will be able to tell you more details about your local regulations.

Type of Tents

Frame Tents are supported by an exterior frame. The center is free from poles.

Canopy - A canopy tent is a simple canvas top supported by four corner poles. It is a relatively small space so it is usually only used to protect guests or food from the weather.

Pole tents involve center poles supporting the tent in the middle and poles holding up the sides.

*Century Tent*s are high-end pole tents. They are known for the dramatic "roof line" full of peaks and valleys.

Other Tents
In addition to the reception tent, you may also need to rent other tents for different functions. A good example of this is a catering tent. Your caterer will need a place to prepare the food away from the reception area.

Tips when Renting a Tent

Tip #1 - Determine the amount of set-up and breakdown time the company will need. Also determine when the construction can take place. Is it the Friday before, the day of, or a few days prior. Also determine when the company will come to pick it up and be sure it is okay with the venue.

Tip #2 - Consider the expected temperature and then decide if you'll need heating/cooling for the tent.

Tip#3 - Know your lighting needs. Is it a night event? If so, does lighting come with the tent or do you need to work with the rental company to rent that as well?

Tip#4 - Comply with safety regulations. Ask if the tent is large enough that it requires emergency exit signs. If so, see if that be handled by the rental company.

Tip #5 - Figure out power. How much power will I need? Is there a source of electricity available? Or do I need to rent a generator?

Tip#6 - Do I need a permit? Plan accordingly.

Tip #7 - If you are considering a tent as a rain plan, what is cut-off date? When do you need to confirm or release the tent? What is the deadline for the company to begin installation?

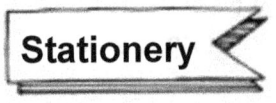 Decades ago, people would actually meet with a stationer (a professional stationery designer) and discuss their options. Today, people just shop online for their invitations and all the accompanying printed materials. This is a lot more convenient, but it means you are left guessing when it comes to some of the terminology. *See the Communicating With Guests section for information on paper and printing lingo.*

In this section, I'm going to help you track down current resources for finding the best stationery options. This means everything from invitations, save the dates, enclosure cards, programs, thank you notes, etc.

In Person There are still privately owned stationery shops and small printers. These shops will allow you to feel the paper options and see examples of what they've done before. It may be a bit more expensive in the long run, but you'll have a much better idea of what you are ordering.

Office supply stores and copy shops are also viable options for your printing needs. Just be aware that their quality isn't always the best, and they aren't the cheapest option.

Craft stores also have print-it-yourself options for purchase. If you go that route, be sure to factor in the cost of printer cartridges.

Online Stores/Marketplaces There are seemingly endless options when purchasing invitations online. A few common places are Etsy, Zazzle, Minted, etc.

Etsy allows you to have highly customizable invitations, and you are likely supporting a small business operation.

Zazzle has a lot of standardized options and routinely has sales to help lower the costs.

Minted provides high quality, well designed options. The price is usually higher than Zazzle, but you get what you pay for.

DIY Printing If you are crafty or artistically inclined, you can DIY this portion of your wedding. I highly recommend that if you have the skills to do so. My go-to tools are Canva and Moo.

Canva is a free, online design program. It is user-friendly, has numerous templates, and gives you access to free stock designs. It is a perfect tool to design a simple invitation.

Moo is a high quality printing service that is primarily used by businesses. Because it isn't targeting the wedding industry, it can provide high quality products at a reasonable price. The paper stock is thick, the ink is stellar, and the printing job is as close to perfect as possible. All that said, the biggest reason I love Moo is its printfinity option. Printfinity allows you to print a different design on every card in a pack. That means you can order fifty postcards, none of them will be exactly alike, and you don't have to pay extra for it.

Of course there are other design programs and online printers. These are just two of my favorites.

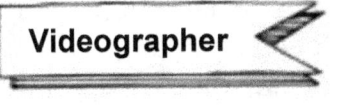

Just like with hiring a photographer, most wedding guides will give you a long list of pointless questions about equipment and such. I'm breaking the trend. Instead, I'll provide you with the steps to hiring the right videographer/cinematographer and how to get the best video possible (in other words, how to make their lives easier).

Tips for Selecting The Right Videographer

1) Find a Video You'd be Proud to Show Off
Do a search of wedding videographers in your area and watch their videos. Select people who have produced videos you would be excited to have for your own; work that you could be proud of. That way, you can point to that example and explain what you like about their work.

2) Don't Skimp on the Price
Remember that with video, you typically get what you pay for. This is not the time to skimp on your budget. I would highly recommend you find someone amazing and respect their price. Great videographers despise hagglers the same way we despise tire kickers at our rentals.

Want a video but don't have the budget? Chances are, you'll find plenty of inexperienced applicants looking to try out this trade. Just remember that you get what you pay for.

3) Get Coffee With Them
Speak with your top choices over coffee. Sure, you can hop on the phone or a video chat, but I recommend meeting in person if at all possible. This is someone who is going to be in your personal space filming you, so it is important that you are comfortable around them.

The goal of this meeting is twofold. One, you determine if you like the person. Two, you explain the scope of the video, what you are hoping to achieve, and determine if they can meet your needs.

Three Questions You Really Want to Ask

1) How do you choose the music for the film?
Music can play an important part in your wedding video. Ask how they choose the music. I've worked with some videographers who create their own music for the video and some who submit requests to use licensed music. Regardless of the route you choose, your videographer will want to work with you to ensure you like the choice of music.

2) What is your backup plan?
If the videographer can't be there for some reason, how do he/she handle it? Is there a second shooter who would step in and take the lead? Do you shoot with multiple cameras? How to you back up your footage? I know it isn't fun, but it's always best to plan for the worst case scenario. That way you know you are all set.

3) How Many Revisions Are Appropriate?
This is an awkward area of conversation, but a necessary one. It is best to know how many revisions they allow *before* you sign a contract.

Remember that videographers want you to be happy with their work. However, they have to put a limit on the number of changes for their own sanity.

Think of it this way. We all know someone who is incredibly indecisive and/or is never happy with anything. Imagine having that person as a client. Yeah... that isn't a good use of anyone's time. That is why there there should be a set limit on the number of revisions.

When working with the videographer about revisions, your feedback should be very specific and thoughtful. Really think things through; explain the what, why and how. Don't just email over a random thought here or there. Be deliberate about your requests.

For more questions you should ask, see the section on photographers.

Give them a break and get better footage

1) Give them space to be creative
It is always advisable to discuss your scenes and the feel of the film beforehand with the videographer. However, on the day of filming it is best to give the film crew the space to be creative. You are paying them to artistically capture your day. Let them do their jobs.

2) Timing
Ill-planned timelines can really impact your videographer. So can the unexpected delays such as traffic jams, hair-and-makeup running late, and impromptu breaks. My advice is to pad your timeline! (See page 183 for help with this) Your day will feel much more relaxed and you'll get better video footage.

3) Unplug Your Ceremony
I know this topic is highly debated right now. You can do whatever is best for you. I'm just letting you know that most of the videographers I've worked with prefer that you have your guests put away their electronic devices for the ceremony. That way they can get a clean shot of your nuptials.

 **Permits/Licenses** While obtaining permits isn't a vendor per se, the permits themselves are typically related to vendor services.

Every wedding is different. Some will require special approval, licenses, insurances, etc. The requirements will vary based on country, region, city, venue, type of event, and services needed.

Use this list as a starting point to make sure you plan for all of the required items:

- Event Insurance
- Liability Insurance
- Alcohol Use Permit/Liquor License
- Food Permit
- Tent Permit
- Approval to use public space
- Special Effects Permits
- Fireworks Permits
- Approval from Police, Fire, & Traffic
- Performance Licenses
- Marriage Licenses

You will also need to plan for any legal requirements in accordance with vendor policies. Policies vary depending on the company and legal requirements vary depending on location. Be sure to check with you company and local authorities to understand the legal requirements.

Vendor Wrap Up

There is one thing I beg you to do — **wrap up loose ends** with the vendors.

If you decide to go with another service, email the others you were talking to. Please don't ghost them! Just tell them you've booked with someone else.

Some people hate this and dread sending the email. I get it. Rejecting others can be hard to do. But rest assured, your vendor is likely used to it and will appreciate that you wrapped up the loose ends. This is business, not dating, so there won't be hard feelings or crying.

If you still can't bring yourself to write that email, here is a simple template for you to follow.

> Hi [Vendor Name],
>
> Thanks for your time and help in discussing services for my [date] wedding. I appreciate your time and assistance. I've decided to go with another vendor and wanted to notify you of this.
>
> Many thanks,
> [Name]
> [Date]
> [Location]

 # Communicating with Guests

Guest Lists
Knowing your target audience is the key to a successful event.

The first step is to identify all the possible attendees for your wedding. Write down everyone that comes to mind. No idea is off the table at this point. For example, immediate family, extended family, close friends, acquaintances, work colleagues, family friends, and so on.

Then it is time to look at the list and begin to narrow it down until it accurately meets your target guest count while still capturing who you want to invite.

How do you decide?
Do you need help figuring out who you should or should not invite to your wedding? Here are a few "rules" to use. Now, please recognize that these rules do not apply to everyone. If you read something and it doesn't apply to you, that's fine. Do what is best for you. These are just some standard guidelines to help you get to your final guest list with a bit more ease.

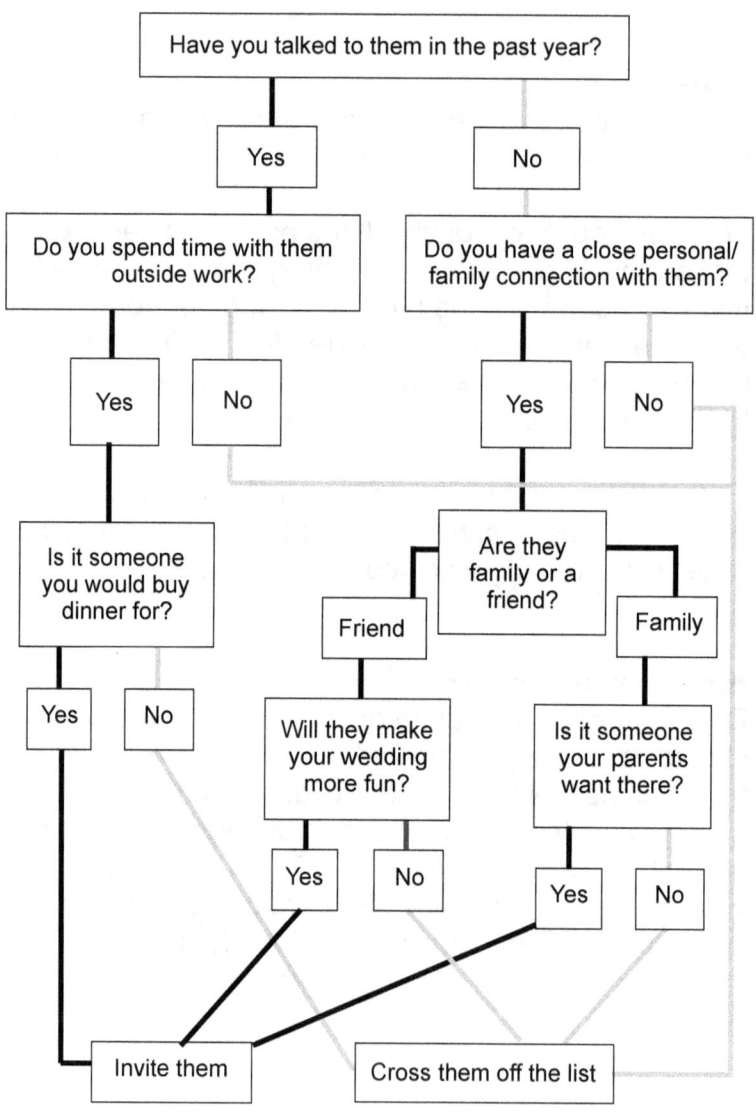

Rule 1: Extended family
The general rule about extended family is that it is all or none. You need to invite all of the cousins or none because if you leave one out it will make for very awkward family relations and it's just not worth it. If you need to cut your guest list, you can cut elsewhere, but if you invite one aunt or uncle, then you need to invite all of them.

Rule 2: Kids
I will tell you that it is not required that you invite children to your wedding. An adult-only wedding is actually standard in the industry. That said, it is a touchy subject. You'll get opinions on all sides telling you what to do.

If children are a big part of who your family is and you feel like you might miss out on having some family members there, then consider inviting kids. Or maybe some friends won't be able to attend if their children are not present. That's something you need to keep in mind when deciding whether or not you want to invite children.

I suggest setting parameters on this rule. Age limits are a common way to do this. For example, only kids 12 and over are invited to sit with families at dinner. The younger kids will either be asked to stay at home or with a babysitter in a separate room. Another way of thinking of things - if kids are young enough to order from the kids' menu, they probably shouldn't have the same meal as the adults.

There are going to be exceptions to the rule. Namely, your flower girl and ring bearer (if you plan on having these).

I suggest you have a very frank conversation with your friends who have kids. Tell them you're going to see a couple kids running around but that they have an active part of the ceremony. Explain that you love them and their kids, but you can't invite all children due to the costs. You are only allowing the kids who are [insert explanation here... family, part of the ceremony, etc.]. You can fill in the details of what fits your situation. The key is to be open and honest about the parameters you set. Be prepared to have conversations with people about your decision.

Okay, say you've decided to go with adults only. How do you communicate that information without being harsh? I suggest writing something like this: "Please grab your dancing shoes and hire a babysitter. We can't wait to see you." Or you can just go online and find what wording works best for you and for your particular situation.

Should I Invite the Kids?

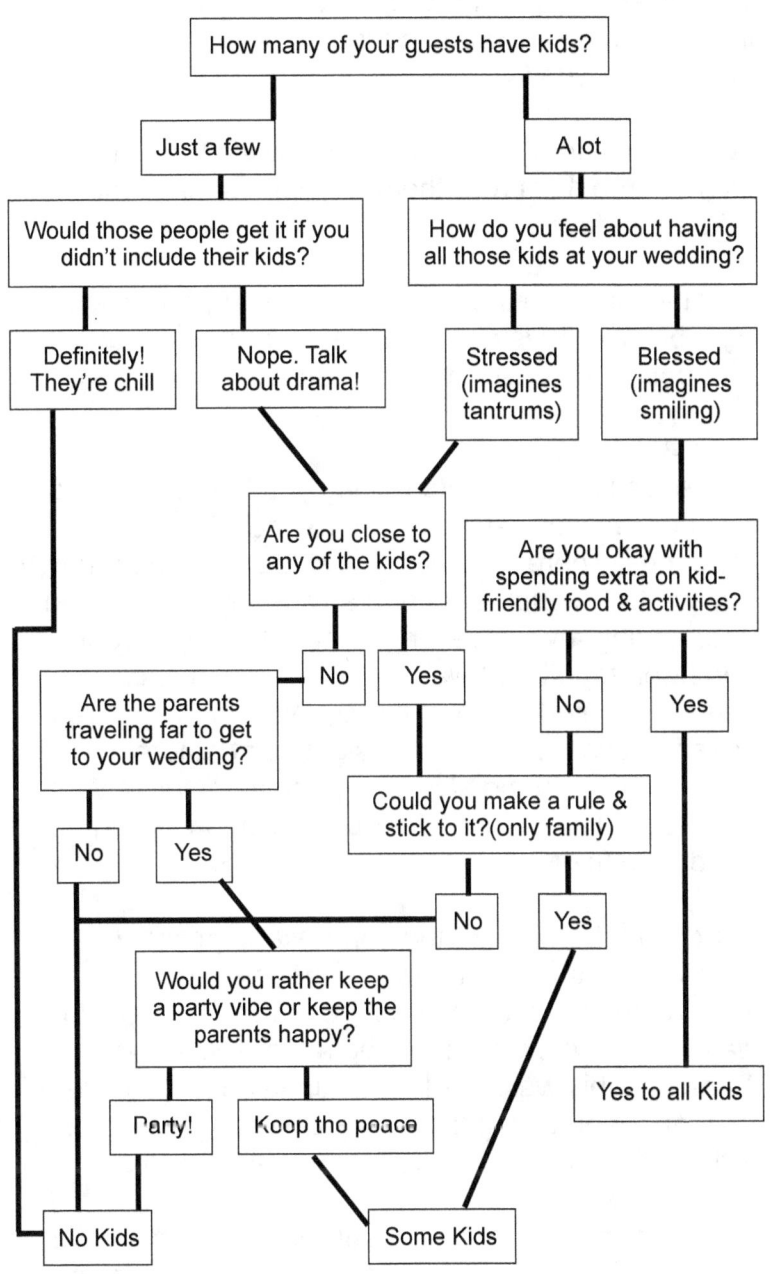

Rule 3: Returning the Invites
One question I get a lot about guest lists is "Person X invited me to their wedding, do I need to invite them back?" It depends...

Was the wedding within the past year? Then you should probably invite them to your wedding and return that favor.

What if you were a part of their wedding five years ago, but you guys don't talk anymore? Then you probably don't need to invite them.

Rule 4: Plus Ones
Some wedding planners will tell you to ditch all plus ones to save space. I've been to one of those weddings. There are a lot of hurt feelings and grumpy guests. I was once invited to a wedding where I had been dating my fiancé longer than the bride/groom had been together. I was invited, but my fiancé wasn't. Granted, most of the couples' friends were asked to come without their significant others. It was just awkward during slow songs. Imagine all of your friends staring at each other blankly and walking off the dance floor...

That might be why I'm the complete opposite. I recommend that you try to give people plus ones if you can manage it. The gesture in itself will go a long way — even if they don't bring anyone with them. Think of it this way, it is like inviting your friend over for dinner and telling them they can bring someone with them. It feels less like they are a third wheel.

That said, plus ones are usually where people cut the list down. The accepted "rule" is that you give plus ones to the people who are in a serious, committed relationship. You can interpret that as you want, but it is usually something like living together, engaged, married, committed partners in a long-term relationship, etc.

You should also consider giving your bridal party a plus one. They are helping you out and putting in a lot of time/money to be a part of your day. Give them the courtesy of a plus one.

Rule 5: Groups of People
Think of groups of people… your coworkers, book club, religious groups, gym buddies, sports team, groups of friends, etc. Make sure if you invite one of the people from that group, you invite the entirety of that group. It'll avoid hurt feelings.

There are some exceptions to this rule. If you hang out with 1-2 coworkers outside of work, then you can invite them and not everyone. Just have a conversation with them and let them know that you're only inviting them and not the entire group; ask them to keep it kinda quiet.

Also, don't talk about your wedding in front of people if they aren't invited. That gets real awkward, real fast. Especially when the time comes and they're checking the mail being like where's my invitation because you let them in on the planning. Now obviously, if they ask questions feel free to answer them. Just don't go on and on about all the fun things you are doing.

Cutting The List: Criteria

Cutting the list down can be difficult and emotionally taxing. Here are a couple questions that I encourage you to ask yourself as you're going over the list looking for people to cut.

Would I take them out to dinner and pay for it?

Because that's exactly what you're doing at your wedding. You are taking them to a very fancy dinner and you're paying about $100 a head. So if you wouldn't pay to take them to dinner then you probably shouldn't pay to have them at your wedding.

Have you hung out with them in the last 12 months? If you weren't getting married, would you see them in the next year?

If you haven't seen someone in a year, you can likely cut them. The exception is if they live out of town. Then the question changes to this: have you talked with them in the last 12 months?

Did they have a major impact on your relationship either directly or indirectly?

If they introduced the two of you, you should probably invite them. Family members should obviously be considered; if they were involved in you being raised, then they had an influence on your life. Your college roommate is a good example of this. You probably wouldn't be who you are today without them. The exception to this rule is if they impacted your relationship negatively. If you don't talk to someone anymore, then don't invite them.

A List vs B List
There are a lot of people who use A Lists and B Lists. This can be useful; I understand wanting to make sure that you invite absolutely everyone you want to your wedding. However, it causes a lot of extra work and requires a lot more brain space thanks to all those pesky administrative details.

Think tracking two different RSVP dates, crossing your fingers you have enough time to send a second run out to friends in time. It's tough to do. Navigating between the two lists is also incredibly difficult to track — even if you are super organized.

I just find it to be an unnecessary headache. It's way easier to manage one list.

Parents' choices for Guests
Sometimes parents will want to add guests to your list. Most couples ask their families' input on the guest list. That said, they can sometimes go overboard with things and want to invite everyone they know (but you don't).

The way to determine this is to rely on who is paying for everything. If your mom is paying for everything and she wants to add people to the guest list, you might need to bite your tongue on this one. It all depends on your relationship and what you can rationally discuss. If you are paying for everything, then you should have complete control over your guest list.

Pro Tip: List Structure

A structural tip for you. After you've put together your guest list, try to group people together. For example, put all your co-workers next to each other or all your friends from one group or another together. This will end up helping you with your seating charts later on. Just think of it as current you helping out future you. You'll thank yourself.

Wrap-Up

Remember, these are not hard and fast rules. They may apply to you, but they may not. They are good rules of thumb to use if you're struggling to figure out where to make cuts on your guest list. That's it for guest lists… on to communicating with guests.

Save the Dates

Save the Dates are standard in the wedding industry but not absolutely necessary. They are used so that people will know long in advance to block off a weekend just for you. They are also incredibly helpful for out-of-town guests who need to have time to make travel arrangements and/or request time off from work.

These notifications do not need to include many details. They can be as simple as the type of event (i.e. your wedding), a date, general location, and possibly even a way to obtain additional information (example: a wedding website).

The purpose of Save the Dates is advance notice. Most people send them out between 6 and 4 months in advance. The industry standard is 6 months for anyone with out-of-town guests and 4 months if all guests are local. I recommend the earlier the better. Earlier notification allows more of your guests to mark their calendars accordingly.

They also force you to finalize your guest list and collect contact information in a timely manner. That way you aren't scrambling to find that information later on in the planning process.

Invitations

The general rule is that invitations to guests should be sent out at least two months in advance. This provides enough time for the invitations to arrive, guests to RSVP, and for you to prepare for the appropriate number of attendees (making enough copies of printed materials, providing the correct number to the caterer, etc.).

That means you should start looking for invitation options a good 4 to 6 months before the wedding. This will give you time to research options, decide on what you want, the printing process, shipping and, of course, addressing your invitations. You can absolutely do this in less time. You could put a rush order ordering online and even have them print the addresses for you. However, the 4 to 6 months I'm recommending will allow for some wiggle room, and I recommend building that in wherever you can. It'll save you tears if something goes wrong.

Paper Invitations (see stationery for resources, etc.) The range of paper  invitations are nearly endless. I could send an entire book just on selecting printed invitations… but few people would have patience for a book like that. So I'm going to make this as straightforward and easy to follow as humanly possible. In the next few pages, there are lingo guides for the format, the paper, printing methods, and a general glossary. After all that we'll tackle envelopes, etiquette, proper wording, and enclosures (aka the other printed stuff you add into the envelope)

Lingo Decoding

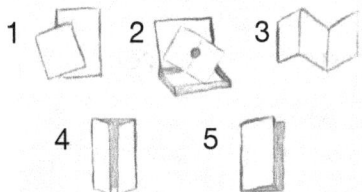

Format: 1-Standard Card, 2-Boxed Invitations, 3-Trifold (3-paneled folder), 4-Barn Door or Gatefold, 5-Bi-fold or fold-over

Printing Processes

Letterpress: letterpress has been used for hundreds of years and is best compared to stamping. The printing method uses blocks with individual letters arranged together in your requested design. The letters themselves are raised metal letters attached to a block. The letters are rolled with ink (only the raised portions have ink) and then pressed with the paper.

Engraving: another printing method that has been around for hundreds of years. It involves cutting the text/design into a copper plate with an acid bath. Then the plate is rolled with ink and wiped off (leaving the ink in the recessed areas only). The printer then places the paper onto of the inked side of the plate and presses the two together. This process essentially forces the paper into the plate and creates a slightly raised design in the end. It can be more costly because of the time-consuming process and because of the higher cost of material involved (copper plate, thicker paper stock, etc.).

Offset or flat printing: the process is similar to what you use with a computer printer, only on a more professional scale. The process is much quicker and the materials are lower quality; therefore, you will pay less for your invitations.

Wedding Invite Wording

Regardless of which route you go, you'll have to choose what the invitation will say. There are hundreds of ways you can announce your wedding on the invitation. Here are a few common wording suggestions:

Couple Hosting

[Insert Full Name] and [Insert Full Name]
Request the pleasure of your company
at their marriage
on [Day], [date spelled out] of [Month]
[Year spelled out]

Couple Hosting - Informal

[Insert Full Name] and [Insert Full Name]
Are starting the adventure of a lifetime
Please join them at their marriage
on [Date]

Married Parents of Bride - Formal

Mr. and Mrs. [Full Husband's Name]
Request the pleasure of your company
At the marriage of their daughter
[First name, Middle Name]
To
[Full Name]
son/daughter of Mr. and Mrs. [Full Husband's Name]

Married Parents of Bride

Mr./Mrs./Ms. [Full Name] and Mr./Mrs./Ms. [Full Name]
Request the pleasure of your company
At the marriage of their daughter
[First name, Middle Name]
To
[Full Name]
son/daughter of Mr./Mrs./Ms. [Full Name] and Mr./Mrs./Ms. [Full Name]

Separated/Divorced Parents

Mr./Mrs./Ms. [Full Name] and Mr./Mrs./Ms. [Full Name]
And
Mr./Mrs./Ms. [Full Name] and Mr./Mrs./Ms. [Full Name]
Request the pleasure of your company at the marriage of their daughter/son

Avoiding it all together

We would love for you to share
this special day with us
as we join hands in marriage.

There are so many options for wording. These are just a few. If you search for wedding invitation wording online, you can find one that matches your situation and desired level of formality.

E-vites
Some people opt to send invitations via email. You can do this through a service like Paperless Post or some other similar services. Those services have built in tracking to allow you to see who has received it, opened it, and who has yet to respond.

Or you can send a mass email from your own email address. My only caution with this option is that your email provider may have a limit on the number of people you email at once or in one day. Or the unusual activity (I'm assuming you don't send mass emails daily) can cause your message be sent to junk mail.

A few years back, there was a lot of debate about E-vites and if they were proper for weddings. That has calmed down considerably in recent years. I say if you are considering this option, look at your options and decide what is best for you. Here are some Pros/Cons to help you get started with that debate:

Pros: It is better for the planet and saves money on postage. **Cons:** It can get lost in the junk mail box. People aren't usually expecting to get a wedding invitation via email.

Enclosures
Enclosures, on the other hand, are a different story. Enclosures are all of the little pieces of paper with additional information enclosed in the invitation. I'll describe the purpose of each one in this section. That said, you should note that most couples are discarding these enclosure cards and have moved towards wedding websites to communicate pertinent information. I'll talk about that a little later.

 **Enclosure Guide**

Maps & Directions Card
These cards help you find the event location. Just as it sounds, direction cards usually provide simple written directions and map cards provide a drawn map. I've found that a combination of the two on one card work the best. Please note that if you include address information on the invitation, this type of card would be redundant.

Accommodation Card
These cards provide guests with information on nearby hotel locations and if there are any room blocks available.

Transportation Card
This card notifies guests of transportation options. It is especially helpful if there is limited parking at the venue or if you've arranged for shuttle transportation.

Rain Card
If you are planning on an outdoor ceremony, this card allows guests to know your rain location.

Pew Card
Pew cards are sent to guests who will have reserved seating during the ceremony. They let guests know where they should sit.

At-home Card (now name-change card)
These were traditionally used to notify guests of where the couple would be living after the wedding. Nowadays, many couples already live together so

there is no need to notify guests of a new address. Given this change in social norms, these cards are being replaced with name change cards. Name change cards notify guests the legal names of the couple after the ceremony.

Rehearsal Dinner Card
These are only included in the invitations of those invited to the rehearsal dinner. They provide relevant information about the dinner (location, time, date, etc.)

Peripheral Events Card
If you are planning any additional events the weekend of your wedding, you can notify guests using this additional enclosure card.

Admission Card
Admission cards are typically reserved for high society weddings that required extra security. They are also used if the wedding is being held in a public space. Their purpose is to help security staff know who they should admit.

Meal Selection Card
This card allows guests to select their meal choice and communicate any dietary restrictions. Many couples opt to combine this with their RSVP card.

RSVPS

Guests use RSVP cards to tell you if they are planning to attend your wedding. Okay, that is what they are intended for which doesn't mean they will use them right away. (More on that later)

Traditionalists will claim that high-bred individuals will know it is proper etiquette for guests to send a handwritten note on their own stationary instead of using the reply card. I call BS on that. Hardly anyone outside the industry knows that trivia tidbit. I had one person do that for my wedding and I work in the industry. Even if people do know about this custom, how many people actually have their own stationery?

In modern day reality, guests will use the RSVP card. It is convenient and has all the necessary information.

Typical wording for an RSVP card is something like this:

```
The favor of your reply is requested by [insert date]

M_____
            ___ Accepts
            ___ Regrets
```

It can be much more playful than this. I've seen couples choose wording like "Hell yeah! Wouldn't miss it" and "Lame. I can't be there" instead of the traditional accepts/regrets.

It is also common for people to use this card to request information about dietary restrictions, meal choices, song requests, etc.

Regardless of what is printed on the card, the return envelope should be pre-addressed and stamped. To cut down on work, you can have those envelopes printed with your return address on them already. Or if you want to save a bit of money on postage, try making your RSVP card a postcard and have the return address already on it.

Even after you've made it as simple as possible for guests to respond, there will be headaches for you. The two big ones are: 1) people not responding and 2) people won't write their names on the reply card. So let's touch on both of those in a bit more depth.

Anyone who has planned an event that requires people to RSVP already knows that people don't tend to RSVP by the date. I haven't documented my clients' numbers, but my guess would be between 25% to 50% of people don't RSVP right away. That's family, friends, co-workers... half of them won't remember to respond. The rest require you to reach out and track down their answers.

There is also the "who does this belong to" guessing game. In other words, a card with no names filled in. I've seen this time and time again with my clients.

 **Pro tip:** Make sure you mark your RSVPs so you know who they belong to. You can write a person's name in invisible ink, fill out the names on their RSVP card for them, label them with numbers, etc. It is almost inevitable that you'll get some RSVPs back without any indication of who they are from. Plan ahead for this and create a fail-proof system.

Website address

Creating your own wedding website is a popular choice these days. It limits the number of enclosure cards you need to print and provides a green alternative to paper. The website gives guests a place to go for answers. They can find the ceremony address, your recommendation of where to stay, other related events, etc. It also allows you to continuously update information as it becomes available.

 **Designing the Look**

Attire
Clothing is an incredibly personal choice. I can't sit here and tell you what to wear and what not to. That would be ridiculous. It is your wedding and you can do whatever feels right. Plus, you've been dressing yourself since Kindergarten. I'm not going to dictate anything for you. What I can do is provide you with the information that will help you better describe the look you are going for.

You'll be faced with explaining your desired style to shop attendants, family, friends, etc. A lot of the lingo isn't used in everyday life and it can be overwhelming when someone starts questioning you about lace patterns or lapel styles when you have no concept of what those things look like.

And that is exactly why this chapter is structured as it is. I'm providing you with a combination of visual style guides and written descriptions of terminology. You can pick and choose the guides that fit your needs. Don't want to wear a tux or suit jacket? Skip that section! Have a specific type of veil you want but have no idea what it is called? Flip straight to there. Think of this chapter as your visual reference guide.

This section will be split according to gender-normative identifiers. I decided on this format because it is what you'll encounter throughout the wedding industry. The industry is still incredibly traditional, but you don't have to conform to these standards if they don't fit you and your future spouse. Pick the section that best matches your gender identity.

Women's Clothing

This section is intended for anyone who identifies as a woman and/or anyone who is interested in finding dresses for any individual in your wedding. This is a largely visual section. It will start with a graph of traditional wedding wear, a section for brides, what to look for when shopping for a wedding gown, bridesmaids, and a number of visual guides to dress elements such as fabrics, lace, dress styles, veils, etc.

General dress code for Women

Person	Informal	Semiformal	Formal
Bride	Simple dress (knee length) No train. Short Veil/ headpiece	Dress of any length. Veil elbow length or shorter.	Floor length gown with train. Veil or headpiece
Female Attendants	Seasonal dress, not expected to match.	Cocktail dress, matching optional	Floor length dresses with matching elements.
Moms	Dress should compliment the other mother's attire.	Dresses just below knee. Outfits should compliment one another.	Long dress. outfit should compliment the other mother's dress

 **Bride** Picking a dress can be a time-consuming process. It can be joyful and exciting, but it can also be stressful and overwhelming. It might be a combination of all those things.

The ideal wedding dress should be a reflection of your style, be appropriate for the location, flatter your figure, be in your price range, and make you feel awesome. Remember, this is the ideal. It doesn't always work that way. Anyone who has shopped for clothing before knows that sometimes you go through dozens of outfits in a dressing room before you find something that fits all these criteria.

In order to help you determine what you are really looking for and help you decode the lingo you'll need to use to find your dress, I've included a number of guides in the following pages.

Waistlines

1-Natural, 2-Princess seaming, 3-Basque, 4-Dropped, 5-Asymmetrical, 6-Empire.

Dress Silhouettes

1- Empire, 2- Ballerina, 3- A-line, 4- Ballgown, 5- Mermaid, 6- Sheath.

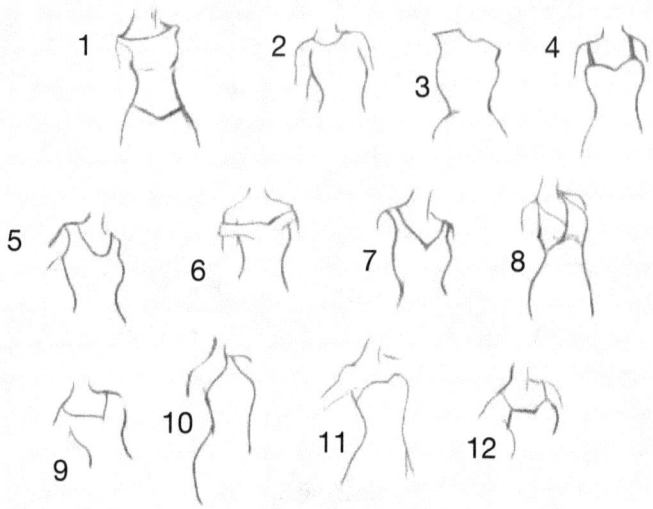

Necklines

1-Bateau, 2-High collar, 3-Jewel, 4-Sweetheart, 5-Scoop, 6-Off-the shoulder, 7-V-neck, 8-Halter, 9-Portrait, 10-Asymmetric, 11-Strapless, 12-Spaghetti strap

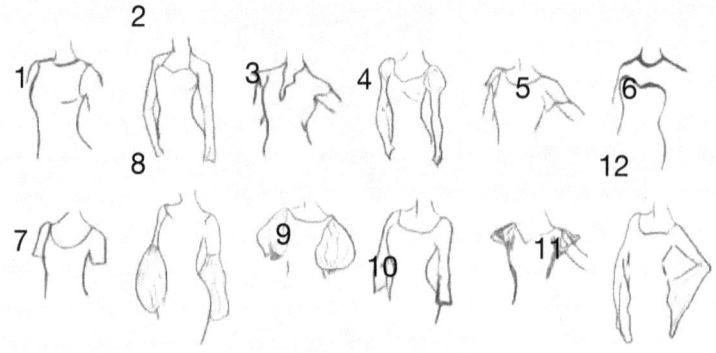

Sleeve types

1-Sleeveless, 2-Fitted, 3-Cap, 4-Leg-of-Mutton, 5-Flutter, 6-Illusion, 7-T-shirt, 8-Poet, 9-Balloon, 10-Juliet, 11-Petal, 12-Bell

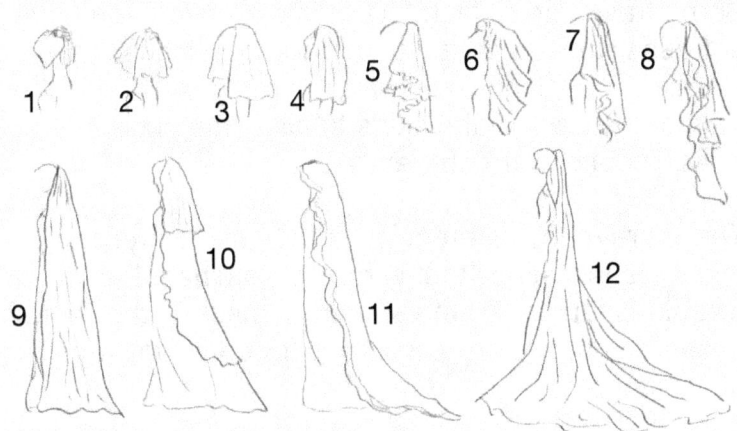

Veil Length
1-Birdcage, 2-Flyaway, 3-Blusher, 4-Fountain, 5-Elbow, 6-Pouf, 7-Waterfall, 8-Fingertip, 9-Floor Length, 10-Waltz, 11-Mantilla, 12-Cathedral

Train Length
1-Chapel, 2-Cathedral, 3-Court, 4-Puddle/Sweep, 5-Fishtail, 6-Watteau, 7-Royal/Monarch

Bustling a Gown
Some trains are detachable; some aren't. If you have a dress without a detachable train, bustling is the standard. Bustling is when you strategically hook the train to the back of the skirts to allow the bride to move around more efficiently.

There are many different ways to bustle a dress, but there are two styles that currently dominate the wedding industry: 1) the standard bustle 2) the French bustle. There are pros and cons for each way of bustling.

- Standard Bustle - This is when the train is hooked, looped, or buttoned on top of the skirt. It creates more folds in the dress so isn't as "smooth" but it is much easier for bridesmaids to manage.

- French Bustle - This is when the train is looped under the skirt. This is considered by many seamstresses the "cleaner" look. It is more complicated to do, so you'll need a really patient bridesmaid.

Regardless of which bustle style you decide on, it is important to have someone learn from the dress shop how to bustle it prior to the wedding day. It can be one of your bridesmaids, family members, or someone who will be there. It is ideal to have that person learning the bustling process in person. However, it isn't necessary. You can also record a video of the process and/or use your favorite video chat application for the training.

Color

While most Americans think of white wedding dresses, many of them are not actually pure white. They are a shade of white. Here are some of the colors you might come across while shopping:

- White - True white is a surprisingly tricky shade. It isn't flattering for a large number of complexions.
- Ivory - Unlike pure white, ivory is flattering for most complexions. It has a creamier, warmer feel. This is like the eggshell of paint colors. It is generally a good fit.
- Champagne - Champagne, also referred to as candlelight, is creamier than ivory and can be almost beige at times.
- Pale Pink - Pale Pink , also called rum, can be either an actual pale pink or a white with a pink cast.
- Colors - The traditional white dress not your thing? No problem. Look for one in your favorite color. You'll likely find a number of brightly color wedding dress options to accommodate all wedding traditions.

Not sure which one to go with? I suggest trying on a few different shades and seeing which one compliments your complexion the best. But remember that different designers may have different hues despite using the same color names.

Dress Shopping Experience

Some brides want an entourage of people to attend their dress shopping experience. This is completely up to the bride and who they feel comfortable having there. If you have a huge supportive family and trust their fashion advice, then go for it.

Just a word of caution: Large groups are rarely in agreement with one another and it usually ends badly for the bride. I've had a client describe it as "having a chorus of opinions that drown out what I really want." Some bridal store attendants are adept at distracting the naysayers and debbie downers so that the bride can effectively try on dresses. That said, I've seen some brides get really disheartened.

It depends on your relationship with your family and friends. If you think your entourage might be a problem, avoid it.

I often tell brides to go it alone or to take only 1-2 highly-supportive people with them. Your family/friends might be upset, but you can explain that the bridal shop prefers you to limit the number. Or if it helps with the credibility, tell them that designer Vera Wang will only meet with the bride alone. No one else is allowed during the consultation.

Tip #1 - Bring pictures of dresses you like. If you like the neckline of one, but not the back of another, point those things out to the sales associate. Try to be as specific as possible.

Tip #2 - Wear undergarments you won't be embarrassed to be seen in. The sales associate will be helping you in and out of dresses during the entire appointment. Uncomfortable with this idea? Wear a bathing suit.

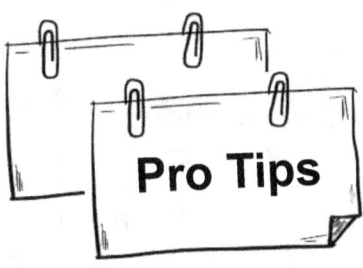

Tip #3 - Bring a camera. If the shop allows photos (not all of them do), you can document your options and get opinions from others. It is also helpful to have a picture of the dress you pick, so you can show others.

Signs of Gown Quality
- Seams are neat and lie flat
- Embellishments are sewn on, not glued on
- Beading or sequins are sewn on individually, not in strands
- Crystals are clear all the way through (Rhinestones have a dark backing which can show up black in photos)
- Inside is fully lined (so that crinoline isn't touching bare skin)
- Zippers are hidden and work smoothly
- Inside of the dress looks completely finished (no raw seams)
- Fabric is matte or lustrous, not shiny
- If it is a structured dress, the corset should be built in with bones that run the length of the bodice.
- Buttons are operational, not just sewn on top of a zipper for show. Buttonholes should be cleanly finished.

 **Bridesmaids** Did you ever watch that movie "27 dresses"? If so, think about the last scene when she makes all the women wear the bridesmaids dresses they made her wear. Some of those were hideous. Never seen the movie? Think about all of the bridesmaid dress horror stories you've heard. Enough said.

In this section, I'm going to go over what you need to consider when choosing bridesmaids dresses. I'm even going to give you some tips on how to make sure your bridesmaids don't hate you because of the dresses you pick.

The key to happiness is low expectations

Lower

Nope, even lower

There you go.

The "Wear it Again" Fallacy
Let's face it. NO ONE is going to wear their bridesmaid dress again. No... no... nope...not that one either. Don't even pretend like it is going to happen. There is only way you can possibly get them to rewear a dress; you ask your bridesmaids to wear the little black dress that is already in their closet.

Now that we've agreed that your bridesmaids are never going to run errands in that floor length gown, let's get down to business.

No single color or dress style is universally flattering. That said, there are some ways to mitigate the distress of your bridesmaids.

Tip #1 - Consider your bridesmaids' complexions. If you have a redhead in the group, don't pick an orange dress. Stick with colors that won't clash terribly with skin tone and hair color.

Tip #2 - Consider your bridesmaids' body shapes. While no dress style is universal, an A-line dress looks okay on most body types. Notice I didn't say fabulous...

Tip #3 - Orange and purple are two of the most polarizing colors. Most people either love them or hate them. There is rarely an in-between. This is why most retailers avoid these colors in their displays.

Tip #4 - Choose a color and let the women pick their preferred neckline and dress style. This will take care of the majority of preferences and body issues.

Tip #5 - Be mindful of the price. If you are asking the bridesmaids to purchase their own dresses, be courteous and don't ask them to spend a large amount of money on a dress. To get around this you can pay for their dresses yourself.

Tip #6 - Consider having dresses made to each person's specific measurements. This will help minimize the need for alterations.

Tip #7 - Order all the dresses at the same time and through the same merchant. It'll be easier to track that way.

The couple's mothers are typically free to choose their own dresses, preferably with the approval of the couple. Some wedding planners will tell you to have the mothers' dresses echo the colors of the bridesmaids. Others will vehemently disagree and say the mothers should be a different color. One thing most wedding planners agree upon is that the mothers should avoid white if the bride is wearing white. Every other color is fair game.

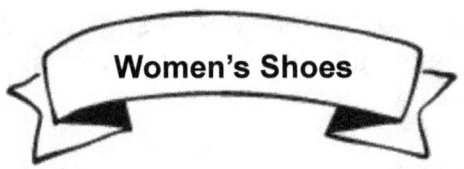

Women's Shoes

Shoes, like clothing, are a very personal choice. That is why I'm going to stick with some tips that'll help you choose.

When choosing shoes as a bride, you need to think about more than what it looks like. Think about how long you can comfortably wear them, what surfaces you are going to walk on, etc.

Tip #1 - If you never wear heels, don't start now. You should choose something you can walk in gracefully.

Tip #2 - Break them in. Don't buy them and leave them on the shelf until your wedding day. Wear them around the house, dance in them, climb stairs. Do whatever you can to break them in now so they are more comfortable the day of.

Tip #3 - If you have a lace hem or have crinoline under your skirts, avoid shoes with jewels and rhinestones. You might love how they look, but there is a good chance they'll catch on your dress. I've seen too many brides trip and/or rip their dresses just because the hem got caught on their shoes.

Tip #4 - If the sole of the shoe is smooth, scuff it up. Create some traction. It'll keep you from slipping.

Tip #5 - Consider the surfaces you are going to be walking on. Heels tend to sink in soft grass.

Tip #6 - Bring backups. Bring along a second pair of shoes so if your feet start hurting you can swap them out and keep dancing the night away.

Tip #7 - Determine if people can actually see your shoes. If you have a shorter dress, shoes will play a bigger role in the overlook. If you have a long ball gown, people won't really see your shoes. Plan accordingly.

Bridesmaids should be allowed to choose their own shoes. You can give them suggestions and guidelines such as a color, closed toed/open toed, etc., but I caution you against telling them to all wear the exact same style. Some women can walk in 3-inch-high stilettos with no problem and others can barely stand upright with a tiny kitten heel. Let them wear what they'll be able to walk and dance in.

Undergarments

Clearly this is a very personal choice. You should wear what is most comfortable to you. However, wedding dresses and formal bridesmaids' gowns can sometimes require undergarments you've never worn and maybe never even heard of. I will simply give you a few tips on how to choose foundation garments that will keep you comfortable.

Tip #1 - Once you've chosen your dress, get tips on undergarments from the salesperson/shop attendant. They know each dress and will be able to tell you what will work best for that particular dress.

Tip #2 - Ask your seamstress to see if foundations (bra, corset, etc.) can be sewn into the dress.

Tip #3 - If you are wearing a ball gown, most everything you need will be built into the bodice of the dress.

Tip #4 - If you are wearing a slimmer dress style, then you should create a smooth layer underneath the dress. It can be an all-in-one, slimmer, or slip. To be honest, this has less to do with hiding any perceived "imperfections" and more to do with how the dress hangs. If there is a smooth barrier between you and the dress, it'll hang correctly and not get caught anywhere.

Tip #5 - Lacey undergarments sound great in theory but tend to show through slimmer dresses. Test what you want to wear with your dress and make sure it isn't visible.

Tip #6 - Strapless dresses can be lovely, but inconvenient for larger-chested women. Make sure you find an undergarment that keeps everything in place no matter how much you move. It sucks if you feel like you have to keep readjusting your dress all night.

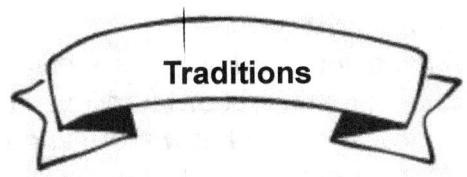

Traditions

Something New, Something Old, Something Borrowed, Something Blue

This is one of the traditions that you can get creative with. There is nothing dictating what you choose for each categories. To help you brainstorm, I've included some of the things I've seen in the industry.

Something New
- Usually the wedding dress
- Rings
- Shoes

Something Old
- Heirloom Jewelry
- Locket in your bouquet
- Grandmother's Brooch
- Vintage car as your mode of transport

Something Borrowed
- Mother's veil
- Family jewelry
- Cake topper
- Coin for your shoe (if you follow that tradition)

Something Blue
- Handkerchief
- Blue jewelry (Sapphire)
- Garter or undergarments
- Shoes
- A blue heart, monogram or date embroidered in the inside of the dress

Honoring your Heritage
One way to make your wedding more your own is to introduce clothing items that are traditional to your own heritage. You'll clearly know more about your own cultural background that I will and will be able to include it in an appropriate manner. Therefore, I'll only provide a few examples. These are all things I've personally seen during my time in the industry.

> **Here are a few ideas:**
> - Tartan sash to represent the Scottish family's clan
> - Indian brides might avoid white dresses (it is not an auspicious color) and choose a traditional red
> - Some Japanese-American brides have turned their traditional kimonos into ball-gown-style dresses. The result is a stunning way to visually honor two wedding traditions
> - Three ribbons sewn into the undergarments or dress of a Mexican bride. The ribbons are yellow, blue, and red and represent food, money, and passion, respectively.

Of course these are just a few of the traditions I've seen during my time in the industry. I encourage you to look to your own heritage and decide if that tradition fits your wedding vision.

Men's Clothing

This section is intended for anyone who identifies as a man and/or anyone who is interested in finding suits for any individual in your wedding. This is a largely visual section. It will start with a graph of traditional wedding wear and a number of visual guides to suit/tux elements such as jackets, shirts, shoes, etc.

Men's Clothing by Role

Men's formal wear is pretty similar so doesn't necessarily need to be broken down based on the role. I'll give you a brief explanation to start and then jump into the visual guides for jackets, lapels, shirt collars, shoes, etc. Also, look out for a few funny side stories about attire choices.

Choosing attire for the groom will set the stage for the other men in the wedding party (groomsmen/ushers, fathers, etc.). It can be a suit, tux, uniform, informal, etc.

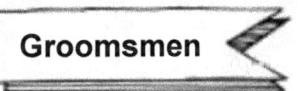

The groomsmen generally dress like the groom, but usually have one element of their outfits that is different. This allows for the groom to stand out visually.

 The Father of the Bride and Father of the Groom usually match the groomsmen. BUT, there is no rule saying that they have to. (See my own story in the following pages)

General dress code for Men

Person	Informal	Semiformal	Formal
Groom	Suit, dress shirt, and tie	Suit, dress shirt, and tie (should compliment bride's attire)	Tuxedo, dress shirt, bow tie, vest/ cummerbund Can also do dinner jacket
Male Attendants	Suit, dress shirt, and tie	Suit, dress shirt, and tie (should compliment groom's attire)	Tuxedo, dress shirt, bow tie, vest/ cummerbund Can also do dinner jacket
Dads	Suit that matches the attendants attire	Suit that matches the attendants attire	Tuxedo that matches the attendants attire

Funny Story...

I mentioned that there is no rule saying that the Father of the Bride or Father of the Groom have to match everyone else. My own wedding was a great example of this. I allowed my own father to wear corduroy pants and a dress jacket. Before you judge my fashion sense, let me explain the story. My dad wears corduroys almost every day of his life. I grew up seeing him go off to work in corduroys, wearing corduroys around the house of the weekend, etc. He even wore corduroys when it was 105 degrees Fahrenheit during the summer. The only time he didn't wear corduroys is when he was going off to soccer practice. So I literally could not imagine him in anything else. The thought of him in a tux or a suit felt strange - completely unlike him. So I decided to tell him he should wear his corduroys and dress jacket, as long as his outfit was color-coordinated with my mom's dress.

You are probably wondering how out-of-place that looked. It worked out fine. Let me give you some visual context. My husband and his groomsmen wore dress pants, dress shirt, vest and a bow tie. None of them wore jackets. My father-in-law wore a suit. And my dad wore his corduroys with a dark blue jacket. Most people didn't seem to mind, especially because everyone who knew him already understood that was the only thing he ever wore. The few people who raised their eyebrows at the decision were told the back story and were usually laughing by the end.

Jackets

1-Single Breasted Tuxedo, 2-Double Breasted Tuxedo, 3-Stroller, 4-Cutaway, 5-Full-dress Tails

Suits

2-Black Tie, 2-Classic Suit, 3-White tie

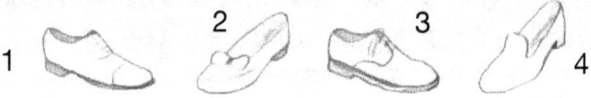

Shoes

1-Oxford, 2-Opera Pump, 3-Buck,
4-Velvet evening slipper

Details
1-Vest (with back) or Waistcoat (no back), 2-Suspenders, 3-Scarf, 4-Ascot, 5-Tie, 6-Bow Tie, 7-Cummerbund

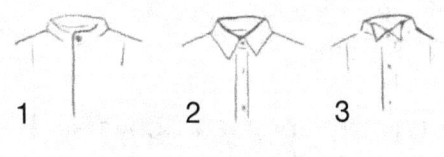

Collars
1-Banded Collar, 2-Winged collar, 3-Turndown collar

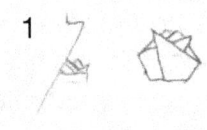

Pocket folds
1-Multipointed with enlarged detail, 2-Triangle, 3-Puffed

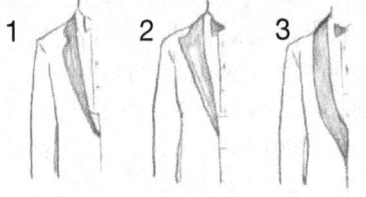

Lapel Styles
1-Notch, 2-Peaked, 3-Shawl

Shoes Cause a Fuss

aka How to make your Future Mother In Law mad

I mentioned earlier in this section that my husband wore rather informal attire to our wedding. He had dress pants, dress shirt, a vest and a bow tie. There was no jacket involved.

When it came time to decide on shoes, there was no question of what he was going to wear. He was going to wear his red Converse sneakers. He had worn his cons to almost every wedding we attended together (except his brother's wedding where his attire was determined for him).

I had no problem with him wearing red Converse. I thought it was hilarious, super fitting given his personality, and flattering because he chose the red ones because I LOVE red.

When we agreed on his shoes, we had no idea how much of an issue it would be. His mom was mad, I mean maaaaaaddd. She gave him a rash of shit (his words, not mine). I didn't realize the extent of this because she was getting on him about it. Then we visited his family a few months before the wedding. I witnessed him getting berated on the subject. At some point I was dragged into the "conversation." I don't remember the exact wording, but the sentiment was as follows:

FH - I wear them to all formal events. Why do I have to wear some uncomfortable shoes instead? Sam, help me out here. You are totally on board with this, right?

MIL - (to me) Are you really going to let him wear something like that during your super-Catholic wedding? It is unseemly.

Me - Ummm... yeah. I don't care what shoes he wears as long as he shows up. Plus, I like the idea. Nothing about this wedding is really that formal (besides my dress).

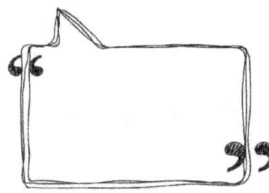

MIL - Oh. You are okay with it? Okay...

I just sit there quietly feeling like my MIL is judging me

The conversation died. However, it has become somewhat of a family joke. My husband had all of his groomsmen wear Converse during the wedding. There were lots of pictures of them showing off their shoes.

Then years later, when my nephew was being christened, my sister-in-law, brother-in-law, nephew, husband (the godfather), and my sister-in-law's sister (the godmother) all wore Converse shoes. The tradition lives on.

...Story Continued

Alternatives
Uniform - Military personnel often wear their dress uniforms during marriage
Informal - Dress pants and dress shirt without a jacket

Honoring your Heritage
Like I mentioned before, one way to make your wedding more your own is to introduce clothing items that are traditional to your own heritage. You'll clearly know more about your own cultural background that I will and will be able to include it in an appropriate manner. Therefore, I'll only provide a few examples. These are all things I've personally seen during my time in the industry.

> **Here are a few ideas:**
> - Kilt made with the appropriate tartan to represent the Scottish family's clan
> - Indian grooms might where a Nehru jacket or other attire depending on the region the family is from.
> - Men with Japanese roots may wear a Haori-Hakama.

Again, these are just a few of the traditions I've seen during my time in the industry. I encourage you to look to your own heritage and decide which traditions fit your wedding.

A cautionary note
Please be aware of cultural appropriation. Try to avoid wearing a traditional wedding costume that doesn't have cultural significance to you and/or your fiancé(e).

Kids Clothing

The ring bearer's outfit is chosen by the couple and traditionally relates to what the groomsmen are wearing. That said, there is a lot of leeway with this. They don't have to match perfectly.

The bride typically chooses the flower girl's dress, but it is also common for the mother of the flower girl to shop for the dress. If you are going the second route, it might be helpful to give the mother of the flower girl an idea of what you are hoping for (think list of criteria, suggestions on styles, and/or level of formality for the wedding). Some couples will choose to pay for the flower girl's dress as a thank you, but that is optional. It really depends on the local norms.

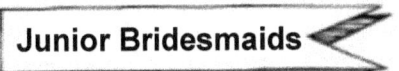

If you have junior bridesmaids in your wedding, their dresses usually relate to the dresses of the adult bridesmaids. Sometimes you can get away with a small adult-sized dress altered to fit. Other times it is better to find a junior bridesmaid dress that is a similar color. When choosing a junior bridesmaid dress, it is important to consider the ages of the girls and make sure the dresses are age-appropriate. It is a good idea to run the choice by the parents of the junior bridesmaid. They might have a different idea of what is appropriate.

> **Pro tip:** Make sure you consider the child's comfort when choosing an outfit. A comfortable ring bearer and flower girl will be more likely to cooperate. If they are uncomfortable, it increases the risk of uncooperative behavior and tantrum-throwing

Another thing is to make sure the kids don't get dressed too soon before the ceremony. The longer the child wears the outfit, the more likely it will get dirty/damaged.

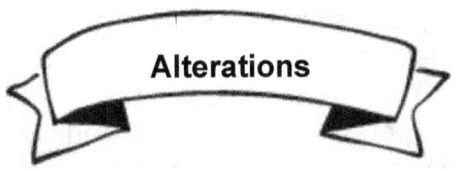

Alterations

Alterations are incredibly important for formal wear. They can make clothing perfectly compliment your body.

Choosing a Seamstress or Tailor
If possible, the garments should be altered where you bought them. This means using the in-house seamstress at the dress shop and the in-house tailor at the men's formalwear store. The reason I recommend this is because the shop will usually take responsibility for anything that goes wrong. Plus, they have experienced staff working on the alterations.

If you go with an independent specialist, I recommend finding an experienced one. Some dress shops and men's formal-wear stores have a list of local professionals. You can also contact the local fabric store to see if they can recommend someone. It is important that you go with someone who has worked with formal-wear on a regular basis. It can require a different skill level and sometimes different equipment.

The Fitting
You'll likely need between 2-4 fittings. The first is the initial fitting where they pin/mark what needs to be altered. The second fitting checks to see if all the initial alterations are correct and if any additional adjustments should be made. If

you are lucky, the second one can be the final fitting. That said, plan enough time for up to four fittings.

Your fitting experience will vary depending on your seamstress or tailor, the type of formalwear you are having altered, the necessary alterations, etc. Since it is an individualized process, I'll give you a few tips on what to plan for:

Tip #1 - If you are wearing a dress, bring all undergarments that you'll be wearing under the dress. Bring the exact ones you plan to wear. That way the seamstress/tailor can adjust accordingly.

Tip #2 - Bring the exact shoes you are going to wear. This will ensure you get the correct hem length

Tip #3 - Skip makeup during the fitting. You don't want makeup to rub off on your gown during the fitting. It doesn't come off easily.

Tip #4 - Have the front of the dress hemmed an inch shorter than the back to help prevent you from catching the toe of your shoe.

Tip #5 - Don't be shy; speak up. Don't like how it looks while pinned or worried about a particular change? Make sure they know!

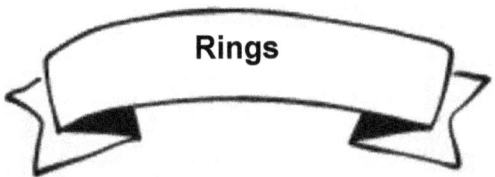

Rings

Wedding bands are another personal choice and should be agreed upon by both parties. Here are a few things to consider when choosing the wedding bands:

- Do you want them to match? It is tradition to get a set of rings that match one another. However, many couples decide to pick wedding bands that suit their individual needs.

- Are you going to have a band that matches the engagement ring and can be soldered together? Or is your band going to be separate?

- Is there anything in your daily life that will dictate what type of ring you need? For example, mechanics may want a ring that is designed to easily break if it gets caught.

- Do you want something inscribed inside the band? If so, you need to make sure the band is wide enough to allow for the inscription.

- Do you want to have diamonds or gemstones in the band?

- Are their any religious or cultural traditions that dictate the rings? For example, Jewish tradition avoids stones in the band because it breaks the circle

Metals

If you plan to wear your engagement ring and wedding band at the same time, it is recommended that you opt for the same metals. That said, it isn't necessary.

My own wedding band isn't the same metal as my engagement ring. They are platinum and white gold respectively. I wear my band daily but rarely wear my engagement ring (only special occasions).

Common options include:

Gold
Tradition has favored gold. In rings, 14- and 18-karat gold make the best choices. Anything higher than that can be too soft to withstand daily wear. There are three "colors" of gold - yellow, white and rose. Yellow gold is the natural hue of the metal. White gold is yellow gold with a bit of nickel to give it its color. Rose gold gets its pink color because it contains more copper and less nickel.

Silver
Silver is not traditionally used for wedding bands. This has to do with the low durability of silver. It doesn't hold up to daily wear. However, it is possible to purchase a silver band.

Platinum
Platinum is rarer and more expensive than gold. It is preferred by some because its cool luster does an excellent job of bringing out the brilliance of a white diamond.

Palladium
Palladium is part of the platinum family. It is natural white and looks a lot like platinum. It weighs less than platinum and costs a lot less too.

Titanium
Titanium isn't considered a precious metal, but its "superhero" status (i.e. strong and nearly indestructible) makes it a viable option for wedding bands. It is a gray color and prized for its strength and light weight. It is especially popular with men who are hard on their jewelry.

There are also numerous alternatives to these common metals. Think wood, copper, rubber, etc. There are even rings designed specifically to break easily to cater to people who work with their hands and risk losing a finger if it gets caught.

Inscriptions
This is a tradition that goes back centuries. It adds something personal to the rings. The key is to keep inscriptions short. The jeweler needs to be able to fit the inscription in a tiny space. If the inscription is too long, it will make it too hard to read.

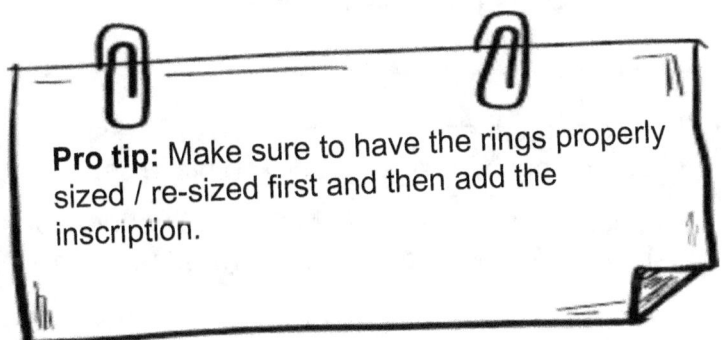

Pro tip: Make sure to have the rings properly sized / re-sized first and then add the inscription.

Finishing Touches

Centerpieces

Just type "wedding centerpieces" into Pinterest and you'll be flooded with options. You can get lost in the endless number of pages full of images. But be forewarned, centerpieces (and Pinterest) can be a rabbit hole. They can end up being a ton of work or much more expensive than you expected. This doesn't need to (necessarily) deter you; it is more of a cautionary statement.

General Centerpieces Ideas:
- Flowers
- Candles (make sure candles are allowed at your venue before setting your heart on this. You can also use battery powered candles.)
- Natural elements in vases (shells, stones, sand)
- Seasonal decor
- Old books (this one is for my fellow nerds)
- Fruit

Regardless of what you choose for centerpieces, there are **two main things to consider:**

> 1. Do the centerpieces fit on the tables while still allowing space between it and the place settings?
> 2. Unobstructed line of sight. Make sure your guests can see each other as well as across the room.

Place Cards
Place cards are small cards that indicate the seat at the table. They are often "tented" paper, but sometimes they are more elaborate. I've seen everything from die-cut butterfly cards perched on the rim of the glasses to prominent tags on the favors. These are, of course, optional. If you don't want to dictate a seating arrangement, you can forgo these.

Place settings
Place settings include the plates, napkins, silverware, and glassware. The table settings you choose will add visually to the table top display. Keep this in mind when choosing your selections. For information on the process of obtaining place settings, see the rental section under "Vendors" earlier in this book.

Colors
Some wedding planning guides will tell you that you need to choose wedding colors. This isn't one of them. Colors are not necessary. Having colors might help with decor decisions down the line, but they are by no means necessary. If you have colors in mind, great. Go with those. If you don't know, don't spend too much time on it. It isn't required. Spent more than five minutes on the colors? Don't waste any more of your time. Do this...

Roll a dice. The number you got corresponds to the color combination below.

1	Blue	4	Green
2	Light Yellow	5	Pastel Pink
3	Red	6	Wine

There you go. That is your wedding palette.

Guest Book

Guest books were originally used to record a list of names and addresses of those who attended. These days they are usually a bit more sentimental than that. They are used to collect messages or record who came to the wedding. It is meant to be a keepsake item. Below are just a few options:

- Customized photo books or scrapbooks
- Note cards and pens to allow guests to provide written best wishes. You can collect the finished cards in a box.
- Have something for everyone to sign. It could be a quilt, thumbprint tree, etc.

The options are endless. My only suggestion is that guests can easily and quickly complete the task.

Favors

Wedding favors should be edible or useful. Most guests won't keep favors with your name and wedding date on them. Obviously, what you provide is up to you, but most prefer something edible or useful. In terms of quantity, the number of favors you order depends on if you are giving gifts to everyone or one per couple. I've found that it is easier to plan one per person so you don't have to monitor the correct distribution of favors.

 **Pro tip:** Always order extra. Be prepared for breakage… or your fiancé eating a few of those customizable candies.

If you prefer to forgo the tangible object, donate to an organization that is meaningful to you two. Then give guests cards saying that you donated money in their name rather than giving them a trinket. You should phrase it better than that, but you get the gist.

Table Numbers
Table numbers help guests identify the tables. Table numbers can be displayed in a wide variety of ways. The key is to make sure they are visible from a distance. This will help guests quickly find their designated table. While it is traditionally numbers, some couples opt for names or themes. The names/themes usually relate to the couple (i.e. places they've traveled, favorite books, etc.)

Escort Cards
Escort cards are the small cards that let guests know what table they are assigned to. They typically pick up their escort card from a table before entering the dining area. They were originally "tented" paper cards. Today the way to communicate the seating arrangements... it can be a board with cards hanging on it, it can be tags attached to favors, or unique card holders (pinecones, old toys, food, etc.)

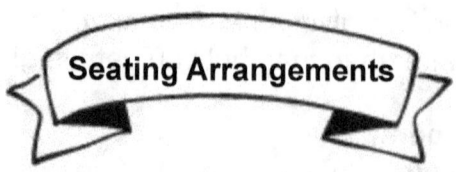

Seating Arrangements

Remember when we were talking about guest lists and how you should group people? This is where it comes in handy. You'll want to seat guests with people who know and like each other (or at least are civil to one another).

Pro Tips

Tip #1 - Allseated is a wonderful online tool to help you plan seating arrangements

Tip #2 - If you can't wrap your head around the arrangement, you might need to go analog. Sometimes physically moving names around helps you visualize things.

Tip #3 - You need to determine the room set-up BEFORE you do the seating chart. It won't help you if you don't know how many people are at each table.

Tip #4 - Don't do a singles' table. That is a good way to make your guests super uncomfortable.

Tip #5 - Make sure you understand people's relationships and history with each other. Don't put people at the same table if there is any chance of a fight.

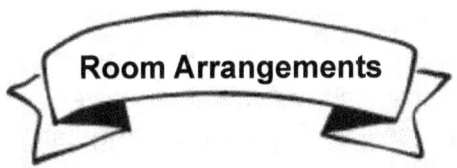

Room Arrangements

Determining how the room will be set up is partly your preference and partly what the space will comfortably allow. It is best to talk with the venue coordinator and rely on their expertise. They will be able to tell you what each option will look like.

With these potential limitations in mind, below are a few common options you'll likely need to decide between.

Head Table
The head table is placed at the "front" of the room and is meant to be the center of attention. Traditionally, this table had the bride and groom seated with their parents and members of the bridal party. The table is sometimes placed on a riser, but this tradition is not currently popular.

Sweetheart Table
The sweetheart table is just for the couple. This is a good option for couples who want to spend a few quiet moments together… which doesn't happen much during the day (counterintuitive, I know).

Round Tables
Event planners will call these either 8 top or 10 top tables. This has to do with the number of people who can comfortably be seated at the table.

Banquet tables
These are rectangular tables that come in 4ft, 6ft, and 8ft. tables. Most venues will have more 6 & 8ft tables on hand. When working with rectangular tables, plan for 1 foot per person. That means you can sit 4 people at a 4 foot table, 6 people at a 6ft, etc. Keep in mind that they aren't that wide. The narrower space can make for cramped place settings and centerpieces. Plan accordingly.

Cocktail High-Tops
If you are having a cocktail reception, you don't need to provide seating for guests. Instead, you might opt for high-top or cocktail tables. They are taller, small tables. They are meant to hold drinks/food as guests stand around them.

Optimal Spacing
Once you determine the type of tables and set-up you want, you'll need to make sure everything will comfortably fit. This is usually taken care of by the venue coordinator. They know their space and can easily set up the room for optimal use. However, if you are DIYing the set-up, you'll need some additional help with this. It is recommended that you leave at least 2.5 feet around each table or 5 feet between tables. This will allow for chairs to be pulled out and for servers to be able to move freely between tables. It is also recommended that you make use of aisles so that servers are not required to move more than two tables deep.

Rectangular Table Setup

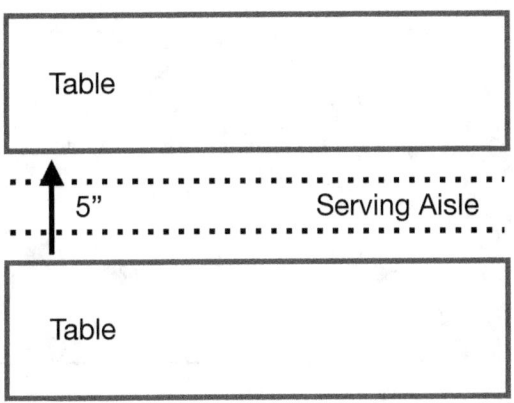

Round Table Setup

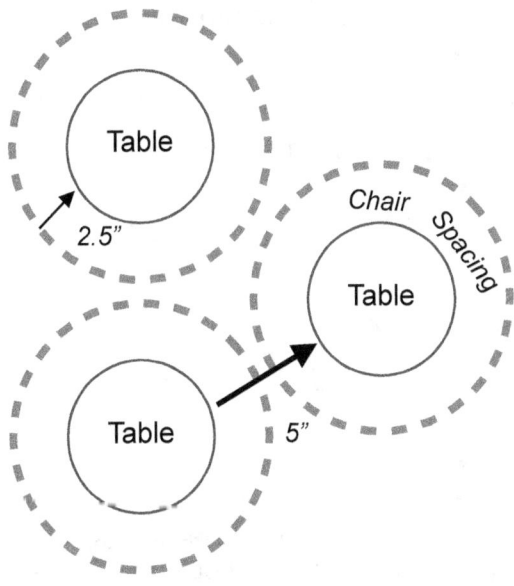

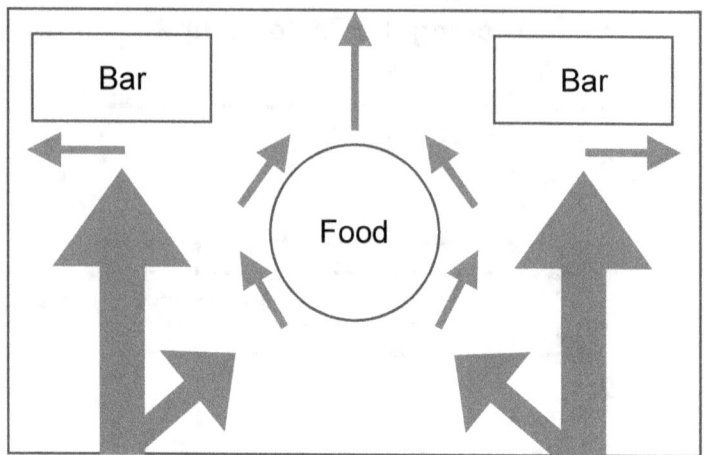

The flow of people should allow for easy access to the bar and food. It should also include a clear path for exiting once food and beverages have been obtained.

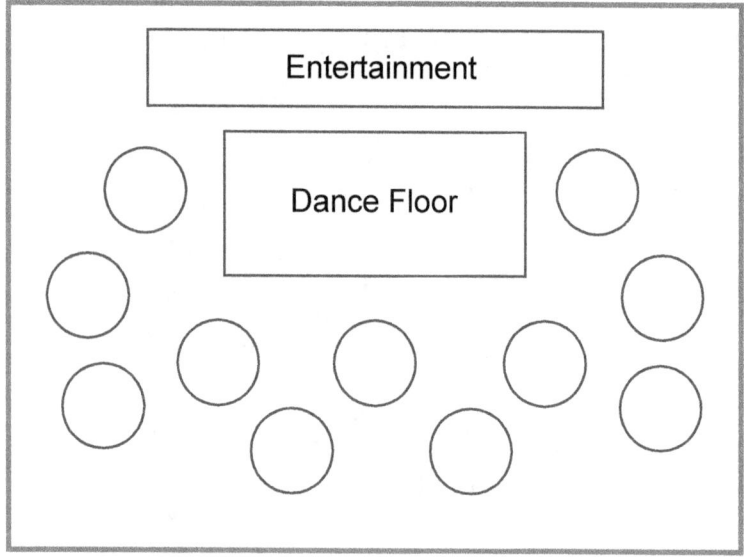

To ensure all of your guests have a decent view, entertainment and dancing should be centered in the front of the room. This arrangement also makes for a favorable impression upon entering the space.

 Creating a Day-Of Timeline

The key to keeping your wedding day running smoothly is to create an iron-clad timeline.
To start, you need to outline all of the essential activities in sequential order. This will start with getting ready and ending with the afterparty. Write it all down in the order specific to your day.

Then you can start allocating the amounts of time required for each. To help you do that effectively, I've decided to tell you about the amount of time you should devote to each activity rather than walking you through an sample timeline with arbitrary times. My hope is that you can start with the ceremony time and build your timeline backwards using the information in the following pages.

Weddings in the United States typically run around 6-8 hours. It is what most vendor packages tend to cover. If you go longer than that time frame, it means you are paying for overtime.

Getting Ready - Hair & Makeup
When it comes to getting ready, the process can vary dramatically. If you are getting your hair and makeup done professionally, then defer to hair and makeup artists for the appropriate amount of time. They'll know best.

For our purposes, I'll give you a ballpark range. Professional hair and makeup usually starts anywhere from five to seven hours before the ceremony. It depends on how many people are getting their makeup done, their hair done, and if you have to travel for that.

This means it usually starts as early as 7 in the morning or late as 10 or 11 in the morning. It all depends on your hair and makeup team, so again rely on them to give you a time estimate.

Of course these estimates are usually just for the bride and bridesmaids (not usually the guys).

Getting Dressed
If you are not doing a first look, aim to get dressed anywhere from an hour to an hour and a half before your ceremony begins. That way your photographer will have time to get all the detail shots — of you getting ready, your shoes, putting on the finishing touches, etc.

First Look
If you are doing a first look, I recommend doing that two hours before your event starts. That way you have plenty of time to get all of your portraits. Be forewarned, your photographer may want two-and-a-half to three hours beforehand, but leave that up to them. I've just found that two hours is the average amount of time for First Looks.

Travel Time: When to be at the Ceremony Site
Make sure to factor in travel time! It is likely that you're getting ready somewhere off-site. Some places have rooms for brides/grooms to get ready. However, plenty of couples get ready off site. Be sure to pad on extra travel time. Plan for traffic, construction and/or unexpected delays. Regardless of how long of a drive

you have, I prefer to have everyone on site and ready to go at least 30 minutes before the ceremony starts.

Here is my reasoning. The first guests usually start arriving around 30 minutes before the ceremony start time. We want the ushers to be in place when the first people arrive.

Ceremony
The Ceremony length is usually anywhere from 15 minutes to a 1.5 hours in my experience. You may have a ceremony that is 3 hours long. It is your ceremony. Just plan for it.

Ten minutes before the ceremony, plan to be in place and ready to start the ceremony. This will help you stay on time.

Start times can be tricky. There are some guests who will be walking in the door just as you are about to start the ceremony. It is best to start the ceremony right at the time listed on your invitation, but sometimes that doesn't happen. There are occasions where traffic is holding up a substantial number of guests, parking is difficult, and/or a very important person is missing. The start time can be pushed back a few minutes to accommodate those late comers; think 5-10 minutes after the time listed on the invitation. Just don't go any longer than 20 minutes past. Remember that 20 minutes would mean that some of your guests have been seated and waiting for nearly an hour.

All that said, make sure everyone knows you are aiming to start the ceremony right on time.

Cocktail hour
After the ceremony, it is customary to send all your guests to cocktail hour. The only guests that don't go to your cocktail hour are your family and wedding party. They need to stick around for photos.

Cocktail hour is just what it sounds like. It is usually one hour of time where you provide guests with cocktails and appetizers. The idea is to entertain your guests before you arrive and the reception starts.

Photo Session
Once your ceremony is over, your family will stay in the ceremony location for about 20-30 minutes for family photos.

Note: This is where a first look session comes in handy. You and your spouse will have already taken portrait photos before the event.

If you have not done a first look, you'll need to take bridal party photos for about 20-30 minutes and then another 20-30 minutes on portraits of you and your spouse.

This means you need at least 1-1.5 hours for photos at the end of the ceremony. It's best to take them in the following order:

1. Family
2. Bridal party
3. The couple

This way you can release each group from the photo

session after their photos are done. Send them to the cocktail hour. It'll keep people happy.

Then it'll just be the two of you with the photographer(s). Once you are done with the wedding portraits, you can head to the reception. The cocktail hour should be wrapping up about the time you arrive. That is the purpose of a cocktail hour. To keep guests entertained while you are off taking photos.

I'd defer to your photographer(s) on this timeline. I never want to impede their art. I just suggest keeping the session to 1-1.5 hours because it is average. It also makes sure that your guests haven't waited around for too long.

Reception
Around 15 minutes before the reception start time, start ushering guests into the reception space. This will give people a chance to take a look at the seating chart if they haven't already and get everyone seated; sometimes it takes a long time for them to move. Regardless of the reasoning, it is customary to have guests heading into the space about 15 minutes before you enter the space.

Grand Entrance
The Grand Entrance is when the couple and/or wedding party is formally announced as they enter the reception room. It acts like a starter for your reception and helps to set the tone for the rest of the night. If this is part of your plan, start gathering the bridal party, family, and anyone joining you for the grand entrance around 15 minutes before. You should be gathering/lining up at the same time guests are going into the space.

Options - First Dance vs Dinner

Some people go from the grand entrance straight into first dance. That is totally fine. Nothing wrong with that. This will take between 2-5 minutes depending on the song.

Other people - like me and my husband - went straight to dinner instead. This is partly because we had to clear dinner tables to make room to dance and also because I know I get hangry when I'm hungry... I'm not a nice person to be around.

Dinner

Dinner should take 45 minutes to an hour and a half. Anything longer than an hour and a half and you can get yourself some pretty bored guests. That would mean that it took 1.5 hours from the first plate to the last plate... and that the first person has been sitting there for an hour with nothing to do.

I would defer to the caterer on the timeframe for this. You can ask your caterer their serving times based on your guest count and dinner type. They'll be able to give you a closer estimate; 45 minutes to 1.5 hours is just the average of the weddings I've worked.

Toasts

Toasts can happen at a variety of times during the night, but it is traditional to do them during dinner. I recommend pre-selecting who will be talking during toasts and limiting the number and length.

First, ask specific people to speak. Don't leave it open-ended. Traditionally, the father of the bride, maid of honor, and best man all give speeches. Some weddings have given more family members and friends the opportunity to talk. I caution you against opening it up to the floor and having just anyone speak. It doesn't usually end well - guests are either bored out of their minds or someone gets embarrassed.

Once you've chosen who will speak, give them a time limit. Tell people to aim for a 3-minute speech. This is the sweet spot. It'll keep people on message and avoid long, rambling speeches. That said, pad the timeline and plan for 5-7 minutes per person. It'll help keep you on track even if someone rambles on for a few extra minutes.

Overall, I'd recommend keeping toasts to around 20 minutes total. People have short attention spans. Twenty minutes is usually the top of the limit. Anything more than that people start getting antsy.

Perfunctory Family Dances
If you haven't done your first dance already, this is a good opportunity to do that. Following your first dance as a couple, it is customary to have perfunctory family dances. This means dances like father/daughter, mother/son, mother/daughter, father/son, brother/sister, etc. It can be the combination that best suits your family situation.

Songs for these dances are usually between two and three minutes. That said, you should plan for five minutes each on your timeline. It'll give you some wiggle room.

Note: If you are in the part of the

world that does dollar dances, this is the time to do those. If you don't know what a dollar dance is, it is basically when guests pay a dollar to briefly dance with the bride or groom.

Options:
Remember you have options. I'm only describing one of the traditional timelines. That said, it's your day. You can do whatever you want, whenever you want. Have cake before your dinner for all I care. It's your wedding; make it yours.

Let me give you an example. My husband and I decided to have dinner inside first. Then we moved everyone outside just before sunset for toasts and cake cutting out on the patio. This not only allowed us to witness a beautiful sunset over the lake, it also gave the venue staff time to clear away some tables to make room for dancing. Oh and did I mention that it also gave people time to eat their ice cream? We had Ben & Jerry's scoop ice cream for guests while we cut an ice cream cake just for show.

Just remember... none of this is mandatory. I feel like I've got to keep making sure you know that none of this is set in stone. You've got options. I know that you know that, but you asked for help on this topic, so I'm giving you some suggestions.

Open Dancing:
Usually when it comes to open dancing, I like to give guests anywhere from 45 minutes to 1 hour for straight fun open dancing before you do anything else you want to check off your list. The reason that I like to allow for substantial time is because a DJ works very hard to get your dance floor moving. You don't

want to kill the vibe after 15 minutes. That would ruin all the DJ's hard work. My suggestion to you would be about 45 minutes to an hour of open dancing.

Or, if you LOVE dancing like me, leave the open dancing to the end so your DJ can build up the momentum at the end and not worry about killing the vibe for things like cake cutting, bouquet/garter tosses, etc.

Cake Cutting/Bouquet Toss/Garter Toss
Some wedding planners will tell you to keep the cake cutting and bouquet/garter tosses until the end of the night to try to keep guests there through the end. If you are relying on that as the only reason guests are staying, you are doing it wrong.

Other traditional advice will have you dance for 45 minutes to an hour and then jump into cake cutting, bouquet toss, garter toss, etc.

I usually tell brides to do the cake cutting, bouquet toss and garter toss towards the beginning (before all the open dancing). This is so that your elderly grandma or cousin with two little kiddos can get home for their bedtimes without missing those highlights. Do you really want a grumpy grandma and screaming kids throughout the dancing? I didn't think so. Make everyone happy and allow people to leave if they don't want to stay until midnight. Plus, it'll mean only the people down to party will stick around - and that vibe is contagious.

Regardless of when you do the cake cutting, bouquet toss & garter toss, you should allot five minutes for each. Five minutes for cake cutting, five minutes for bouquet toss, and five minutes for garter toss.

Last Call
At the end of the night, the bar will have last call. Last call is usually 15 to 30 minutes before the end of the event. Usually the bar service or catering company will tell you what time that should be. Sometimes your venue will also request it at a certain time. Once that time is predetermined, either you or a representative will ask your DJ/band to announce last call at that time.

Your Exit
Some people will do a "Send Off" or Grand Exit at the end of the reception. If this is the case, ask your guests to line up 10 minutes before the end of the reception. I say 10 minutes because it'll take some time for people to gather their things and get in line.

Pro Tip: Designate someone to explain what guests are expected to do. Also designate someone to pass out any necessary props.

Pro Tip: Make sure to clear the details of the send-off with your venue. You don't want to purchase hundreds of sparklers just to have your venue veto the idea because it is against their fire code.

If you want to let the party come to an end without an organized send-off, that is fine too, you can plan to skip this part. Whatever you want.

Overview

So that's it; some guidance on what your day-of timeline could look like and the average times for each activity. Regardless of what your day looks like, it is important to write down the proposed timeline.

The reason that we create a day-of timeline is because we want everything to flow seamlessly from one event to the next. We never want you or your guests to feel like something is wrong. A timeline will provide a good cadence for the day.

Pro Tips for making the day run smoothly:

1) Write out the timeline and distribute it to everyone involved in the planning and/or implementation of the event.

2) Delegate! Delegate! Delegate! Make sure there is someone responsible for each task and portion of the day. Then document who is responsible for each function and let the vendors know. In theory, this should take some stress off your shoulders.

3) Add in extra time wherever you can. Consider worse case scenarios for travel times to accommodate traffic or add in 10 minutes between each activity. This padding will help you stay on track.

Sample Timeline

I've already told you about the amount of time you should devote to each activity. My hope is that you can start with your ceremony time and build your timeline up and back using the information I provided.

Just in case you still feel lost and would benefit from an example, I've included a sample timeline with arbitrary times.

SAMPLE WEDDING DAY SCHEDULE

Time	*Activity and events*	*Parties involved*
9:00 – 1:00	**Wedding party gets ready and photo sessions**	**Couple & attendents**
9:00 am	Hair and makeup for Bride & Bridesmaids.	Bride & Bridesmaids
11:00 AM	Bride and Bridesmaids eat lunch	Bride & Bridesmaids
	Groom and groomsmen eat lunch	Groom & groomsmen
11:30 AM	Bride and bridesmaids get dressed	Bride & Bridesmaids
	Groom and groomsmen get ready	Groom & groomsmen
11:45 AM	Groom individual portraits	Groom
12:00 PM	Groom and groomsmen portraits	Groom & groomsmen

Time	Activity	Who
12:15 PM	Bride individual portraits	Bride
12:45 PM	Bride and bridesmaids portraits	Bride & bridesmaids
1:00 – 2:30	**First Look**	**Bride & groom**
	Groomsmen decorate the car	Groomsmen
1:00 PM	The couple gets ready	Bride & groom
1:15 PM	First Look	Bride & groom
1:30 PM	Couple's Wedding Portrait session	Bride & groom
2:15 – 3:30	**Arrivals & Set-up**	**All parties involved**
2:15 PM	Ushers arrive at church Musicians arrive at church	Ushers Ceremony musicians
2:30 PM	Ceremony Portraits	Family & Couple & Wedding Party
2:45 PM	Family, Officiant, flowers girls, ring bearers arrive Pianist arrives Greeters and readers arrive and set up	Fmaily, Officiant, flower girls, ring bearer, pianist, greeters, readers
3:30 – 3:55	**Final preparations**	**Wedding party, parents**
3:30 PM	Wedding party to dressing room	
3:55 – 5:15	**Wedding ceremony**	**All**
3:55 PM	Prelude	Musicians

Time	Event	Who
4:10 PM	Ceremony service starts	All
5:15 PM	Ceremony service concludes	All
5:00 – 6:15	**Reception set up, ceremony site cleanup**	**Reception greeters, attendants**
5:00 PM	Reception greeters and attendants leave	Reception greeters, attendants
5:15 PM	Wedding party and Family leaves immediately for reception site	Wedding party, Family
6:15 – 7:00	**Wedding party arrival and preparation for grand entrance**	**Couple, wedding party, & parents**
6:15 PM	Couple, wedding party, immediate family arrive	Couple, wedding party, & parents
6:45 PM	Wedding party and immediate family form reception line to great guests as they arrive.	Couple, wedding party, & parents
7:00 – 12:00	**Reception begins**	**All parties**
7:00 PM	Grand entrance	Couple, parents, & wedding party
7:15 PM	Dinner begins. Couple served first.	All
7:30 PM	Toasts by parents, best man, and maid of honor	Parents, Best Man, Maid of Honor
8:15 PM	Couple to do table visits	Couple & photographers
8:45 PM	Cake cutting	Couple

Time	Event	Participants
9:30 PM	Couple's first dance	Couple
9:35 PM	Family Dances	Parents, Couple
9:45 PM	Bouquet toss & Garter Toss	All
10:00 PM	Dancing begins	All
11:50 PM	Guests gather for Send-Off.	All
12:00 AM	Send off	All
1 AM	Afterparty	All

Want to see my own wedding schedule? It's 25 pages and available for download on my website.

Planning Timelines and Checklists

You'll come across a number of generalized timelines and checklists. I've even included a 3-month example in the coming pages.

That said, you should make every effort to personalize your timeline and checklists.

Start with the date most conducive to your needs and circumstances. How much time is there between now and your wedding?

Use this information to create a personalized timeline. Work backward to establish a realistic, week-by-week activity plan.

Then use this plan as a touchstone to track the planning process.

Sample 3 Month Timeline

90 Days
- Decide on a general vision
- Book a site and set a date (do this ASAP since many venues book a year or more in advance)
- Create a budget
- Compile a guest list
- Invite your guests (evites or paper invites)
- Decide on outfits for you, your partner (to allow for alterations if necessary)

Optional:
- Start a website
- Set up registry
- Pick bridal party/groomsmen/attendants and tell them what to wear
- If you are staying closer to the wedding site, make the appropriate arrangements

80 Days: Vendor hiring
- Come up with a list of potential vendors for each service
- Ask for quotes from potential vendors. To save time, be sure to include all relevant information in the initial email
- Decide on and hire vendors

60 Days:
- Make a ceremony plan
- Hire officiant or ask someone close to you to get trained/certified as an officiant.
- Buy wedding rings (if you are having them).

Optional:
- Honeymoon flights, accommodations, etc.

- Plan rehearsal dinner (traditionally the groom's family plans this, but today anything goes. Feel free to be as involved in this as your situation warrants).

50 Days:
- Check in with wedding vendors and finalize details
- Track down RSVPs and finalize guest list
- If you are doing a seating chart, start on that
- Start working on any "paper" items you'll use that day (programs, menus, place cards, etc.)

40 Days:
- Continue working on any uncompleted steps above.
- Ask people doing toasts to give speeches. This will allow them time to start preparing them.

20 Days:
- Touch base with vendors (confirm details with them, arrange final payments, delivery location and times, etc.)
- If you are doing gifts/favors, buy them. (This includes wedding favors, gifts for the attendants, gifts for your parents, and for each other.)

10 Days:
- Create a day-of schedule and contact list
- Delegate day-of tasks to trusted friends/family members/event staff (get their consent of course)
- Distribute event plan to parents, attendants, and all vendors.
- Give vendors final guest counts

Optional:
- Apply for marriage license
- If you are staying elsewhere during the wedding, pack your bags

- Put cash tips for vendors in labeled, sealed envelopes and give to a person designated to distribute them.

Day Before:
- Rehearsal
- Rehearsal meal
- Any necessary set-up/decoration

Day Of:
- Get Ready, Get Set & Get Married.

Follow up:
- Clean up and pick up items from venues
- Email vendors & thank them for their help
- Send thank you cards for wedding gifts
- Settle up any final bills

Optional:
- If you had photographers/videographers, work with them to receive final product
- Donate flowers/decorations to a local nursing home or hospital.

 # 9 Post-Event Wrap-Up

The reception is over and the guests are filing out. You can breathe a sigh of relief. It's over. Now all that is left is a few loose ends to wrap up after the event.

Clean Up

One of the wrap-up activities is clean-up. Actually it is the first thing to do. This should be either the night of the reception or the next morning. It depends on the venue and their preferences. Some will ask you to finish cleaning that night while others will allow you to store a few things until the next morning. Work with the venue's site coordinator to determine what you are responsible for and what they will take care of. Below are a few things to consider for a quick and efficient clean-up so no one is stuck at the venue for hours after the party ended.

Designate a cleaning team

Avoid surprising people with last minute clean-up duty. Designate a clean-up team long before your reception. The head event planner will meet with the pre-designated cleaning team and delegate tasks. This ensures that everyone is doing their part and all the cleaning is completed in a timely manner.

Pro Tips for Clean-Up Team

Appoint people (wedding party, parents, siblings, etc.) to do the following:

- Make sure nothing is left in the changing rooms
- Transport gifts to the car or bridal suite
- Collect cash from money dance or checks from the box on the gift table
- Put valuables in a hotel safe or other secure place
- Take the top tier of the wedding cake home to freeze
- Take home personal items (cake-cutting knife, toasting flutes, guest book, decorations, etc.) Make a list ahead of time so they know what to collect
- Save and take home sentimental items (seating card, bouquets, etc.)

Have someone supervise the cleaning team

In addition to the cleaning team, it is important to designate a lead person. I recommend someone who has had experience managing people and delegating tasks. If you have an event planner, ask him/her to coordinate this. If it is your family/friends, designate someone who is organized and isn't afraid to ask for help.

It is important for the lead person to stay the entire length of clean-up. Supervising the closing activities may consist of thanking vendors, coordinating the cleaning team, providing payment, etc. The lead person will also see that everything is complete at the end of the day.

Coordinate with Vendors
Get clear on who is responsible for what. Don't assume everything will be taken care of by the venue or caterer. To help you determine who will help with clean up ask the key players a few questions.

Venues

- Do you provide staff for clean-up purposes? If so, what tasks are they responsible for?
- Are you responsible for trash and recycling disposal? Or do you require us to take care of disposal?
- Can we store items in a secure room overnight? Or do we need to remove all personal belongings that evening?
- When does the space need to be clean? Can we come back the next morning to clean? Or does it need to be that evening?
- (If you've used their tables/chairs) Will your staff be responsible for the break-down of tables and chairs?
- (If rented items) Are there restrictions on when the rental company should coordinate pick-up?

Bar

- Do you provide staff for clean-up purposes? If so, what tasks are they responsible for?
- Are you responsible for trash and recycling disposal? Or do you require us to take care of disposal?

- (If you've rented glasses from an outside company) Do you handle the return of the glassware?
- Will you be breaking down the bar area and putting away furniture?

Catering
- Do you provide staff for clean-up purposes? If so, what tasks are they responsible for?
- Are you responsible for trash and recycling disposal? Or do you require us to take care of disposal?
- (If you've rented dishes/glasses/linens/etc. from an outside company) Do you handle the return of the rented items?

Miscellaneous Paperwork

☐ **Submitting marriage license**
One piece of important paperwork is the marriage license. In most cases, your officiant will mail the license to the required state/county/town office. Your official license should arrive in the mail in a few weeks.

☐ **Notifying Companies**
You'll need to update information and marital status with a number of companies once you are married. While the list of places will be individualized to you, below are a few things to consider.

In general, there are two tasks to complete:
- Update any account that requires a beneficiary. Even if your spouse was already listed, have them update your relationship status.
- Update any emergency contact information. Even if your spouse was already listed, have them update your relationship status.

Things to Update:
- Insurance plans (health, home, car, life, etc. Add a rider to cover your rings)
- Wills (if you have one. If you don't, consider creating one)
- Medical records (emergency contact)
- Investments (beneficiary)
- Retirement accounts (beneficiary)

- Bank accounts (beneficiary)
- Employer paperwork

📑 Name Change Paperwork (Women)

If you decide to change your name, you can start on that paperwork once you've received your marriage certificate in the mail.

Be aware that you'll likely need a few official copies of your marriage license for this process. I suggest getting anywhere between three and five official copies. This is because the DMV, Social Security Office, and Passport Agency will likely want an original/certified copy of the marriage license to be submitted with the paperwork. They don't typically accept photocopied versions. And, of course, you'll want to keep a copy for yourself.

Social Security:
When starting the name-change process, start at the Social Security website. They have instructions on how to request a card under your new name. You'll need your old Social Security card and your marriage license for this process.

Pro Tip: Be aware of any companies offering to go through the process for a price. This process should be free.

DMV:
The next step is to change your name on your driver's license. I'm tempted to start cracking DMV jokes, but I bet you have a few yourself. Start thinking sloths.... And go...

I could tell you everything you need to bring with you to your DMV or to make an appointment to help skip the enormous line. But we all know how futile that would be. Check with your local DMV and see what they need for paperwork. Then be prepared to bring 12 other forms of identification just in case the regulations changed by the time you get through the line (true story... definitely happened to me in Maryland).

All joking aside, you'll also need to think about your car registration and title. I recommend bringing all the necessary documentation for that process as well. It is better to get it all done at once.

Passport:
You also need to change your name on your passport. Currently, you can access the passport name change form online. You can also pick up the form at the post office. You'll have to mail the form in with your current passport and a certified copy of your marriage certificate.

Name Change Paperwork (Men)

I wish I could say that the process for name changes was exactly the same for men. It isn't. Due to the traditional origins that surround the practice of name changing, the systems aren't set up with men in mind. They assume that the only people changing their names after marriage are women.

The laws vary by state, but some will require you to petition the court to legally change your name. Others, like New York, actually allow men to enter a new surname on their marriage license and go through the same process as women.

Final Payments

After the wedding is over, you'll likely have a few remaining bills to pay. Remember this might include bills from your caterer or bartender whose charges might vary based on the quantity consumed. You should expect these bills as you will have already agreed to them in your contract(s) with vendor(s).

> **Pro Tip:** If you are going on your honeymoon directly after the wedding, make sure your vendors know. That way they won't worry if you haven't immediately responded to their request for payment.

Regardless of what your final payments are, I suggest you pay them promptly. Be respectful of their time and stay on top of those loose ends.

Thank You Notes

After your wedding, you'll want to express you gratitude to everyone who participated in your wedding. Hand-written notes are rare these days, so I recommend taking the time to hand write your messages of gratitude.

Family
Show your family (both yours and your in-laws) some heartfelt thanks by writing a hand-written note to thank them for participating in your celebration.

Wedding Party
The same goes for your wedding party. Thank each of them individually for their participation in the wedding.

Vendors
Don't forget your vendors. Remember to say thank you to them too, they helped you celebrate and provided you with a service. Thank them for it!

Guests
Thank your guests for celebrating with you and for any gifts they gave you. I recognize writing hand-written notes for all your guests can seem like a daunting task, so here are a few tips:

Tip #1: If you have been receiving gifts off your registry throughout the year, write the gift thank you note immediately after receiving the gift. This will allow you to spread out the work.

Tip #2: Send a wedding announcement as a way of thanking people for attending. It isn't as personalized, but you can still add a quick hand written note on the card.

Tip #3: Check out the free guide to writing Thank You notes on my website. It'll help you keep the notes interesting and heartfelt. Avoid a robotic message, as there is nothing grateful-sounding about that.

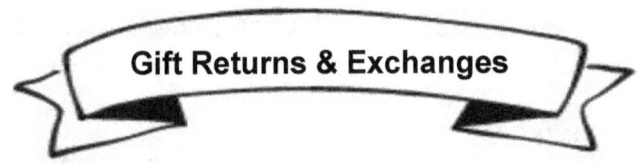

Gift Returns & Exchanges

The rise of registries has drastically reduced the need for gift returns and exchanges. Guests will know exactly what you want and if a gift is already purchased. These days it is doubtful that you'll have duplicate toasters. That said, sometimes you'll still need to return or exchange a few items.

I recommend doing returns/exchanges within a month of the wedding. Some stores have a strict 30-day return policy while larger chains will have a 90-day return policy. Some stores, especially those you have registries through, have wedding-specific policies. This means if someone purchases you a gift off your registry, they are more lenient with their return timelines. Check with individual stores for their specific policies.

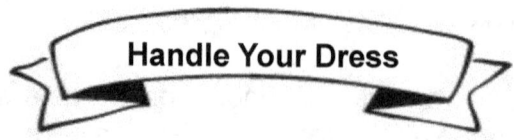

Handle Your Dress

Your wedding day is over and now you aren't sure what to do with your dress. Below are a few pieces of conventional wisdom. You can choose what works best for you.

Cleaning
The first step is to clean the dress. If there are visible stains on the dress, get it to the cleaner's right away (within a day or two). If there aren't any stains, you can wait a few weeks. Whatever you decide, get it to the cleaners within six weeks.

Preserving
If you choose to preserve your dress, this can be done through select cleaners and bridal shops. The process entails placing the clean gown in a pH neutral, acid-free box and stuffed with acid-free white tissue paper. This is the best way to keep the dress from deteriorating over time.

Storing
Regardless of if you have the dress preserved or cleaned, there are some guidelines for storing your dress. Store it in a dry location, away from direct sunlight. Also avoid extreme changes in temperature.

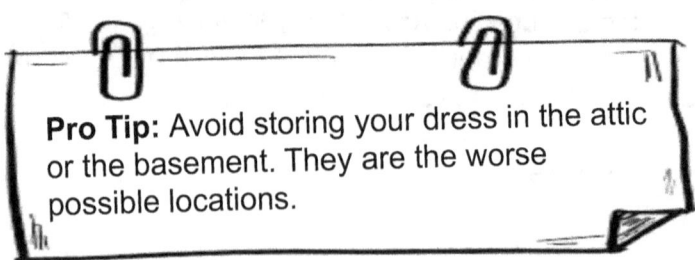

Pro Tip: Avoid storing your dress in the attic or the basement. They are the worse possible locations.

I recommend storing your dress in the closet or under the bed. The reasoning behind this suggestion is simple: any room you are living in will be kept within a reasonable temperature range and humidity level.

Donating
If you don't want to keep your dress or would prefer that it goes to a good cause, consider one of these options:

- Wish Upon A Wedding (provides gowns for terminally ill brides)
- Angel Gowns (dresses are turned into burial gowns for infants)
- Brides Across America (provides gowns for military brides)
- Wedding Recycle Groups on Facebook (give your dress to someone local)
- Thrift stores that benefit charitable causes you support

Returning Rentals

Men's Rental Clothing
If the men involved in the wedding rented a tux or suit, make sure they are returned the next day (or within the timeframe prescribed by the shop). There are two general approaches to this: 1) designate one person to return all the rentals at once, or 2) have people return their own rentals. It is up to you.

Women's Rental Clothing
If women rented clothing from an online service such as *Rent The Runway*, have them return the items in a timely manner. Given the nature of these services, it is best to have individuals return their rentals via mail the next day (or within the timeframe prescribed by the company).

Other Rentals
Chances are that you've had to rent something from a wedding rental company. It could be a tent, dishes, glasses, furniture, linens, etc. You should arrange pick-ups with the company you rented from and coordinate that with the venue. Most companies will want the items returned either the next day or the next business day. Most venues expect this and will have someone on site to facilitate this. However, it is always good practice to confirm that the rental company and venue site coordinator have similar expectations for when rentals will be picked up.

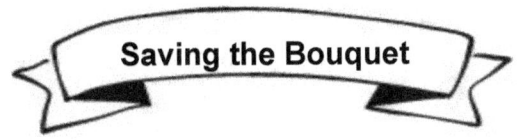

Saving the Bouquet

If you decide to save your bouquet, there are a number of options. You could have it professionally preserved using a local service, dry it yourself or press the flowers. Below are a few common options with brief explanations.

Air-drying
To air dry, hang the bouquet upside down in a dry, dark place. The drying time will vary but is typically between 1-4 weeks.

Pressing
Place the individual blooms in a flower press or between the pages of a heavy book. Once pressed, flowers can be arranged and displayed as desired.

Freeze-drying
This method is done by professionals and is the most effective way to have flowers maintain their 3-D shape. The process involves having the flowers flash-frozen and then reheated to room temperature over a four-week period. The bouquet is then kept under glass.

Freezing the Cake

It is tradition to freeze the top tier of your wedding cake and eat it on your first anniversary. If anyone has left something in their freezer for a full year, you know what freezer burn looks and tastes like. To help maintain the taste and texture of the cake, try the following tips:

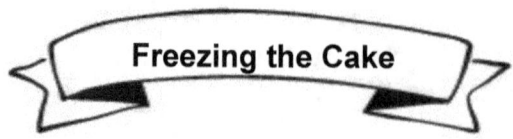

Tip #1 - Remove any sugar flowers. They don't freeze well.

Tip #2 - Set the cake in the refrigerator overnight to harden the icing. This will help prevent the plastic from sticking.

Tip #3 - Vacuum seal the cake, if possible.

Tip #4 - If you don't have the ability to vacuum seal, be sure to use multiple layers. Use two layers of plastic wrap, followed by a layer of aluminum foil.

Tip #5 - Place the wrapped cake into a hard plastic or glass container to prevent it from getting smooshed by the heavier items in your freezer. Be sure to label it too.

Once you are ready to eat the cake, take it out of the freezer and move it to the refrigerator to defrost. Keep it in its wrapping as it defrosts. It is best to let it fully defrost in the refrigerator and then let it warm up to room temperature. A quick warning: taking it straight from the freezer and letting it defrost at room temperature will increase the chances of condensation on the frosting.

Follow Up

Follow up with Photographer and Videographer
It'll likely take some time for the photographer and videographer to provide you with the final product. Don't expect the images right away. I know you are excited to see them, but editing the end product isn't a quick job.

The average wait time for photos and videos is typically between 2-6 weeks. The time it actually takes will vary depending on the photographer, their schedule, how many photos they took that day, how much editing each photo needs, etc.

Many photographers and videographers will try to send you a sneak peak early on and then the finished product at a later day.

If you start feeling frustrated that you haven't gotten back the final product yet, remember that the photographer and videographer usually spend much more time editing the images than they do capturing them. Both are working hard to create that finished style you hired them for.

My advice: Determine how long it'll take *before* your wedding and follow up with them when it nears that expected date. It'll be worth the wait. Be patient in the meantime.

 # Wrap Up of the Wrap Up

Congrats! You've done it. You've gotten all the way through planning, you got married, and you have everything wrapped up. It's been an honor to take this journey with you.

I'd like to propose a final toast to you: "May your love be modern enough to survive the times and old-fashioned enough to last forever."

www.ingramcontent.com/pod-product-compliance
Lightning Source LLC
Chambersburg PA
CBHW050200130526
44591CB00034B/1449